I0795185

The Most Wonderful Terrible Person

The Most Wonderful Terrible Person

A MEMOIR OF MURDER IN THE GOLDEN STATE

DEBRA MILLER

SHE WRITES PRESS

Published in 2026 by
She Writes Press, an imprint of The Stable Book Group

32 Court Street, Suite 2109
Brooklyn, NY 11201
https://shewritespress.com
Library of Congress Control Number: 2025927609
ISBN: 979-8-89636-102-2
eISBN: 979-8-89636-103-9

Interior Designer: Tabitha Lahr

Printed in the United States

Names and identifying characteristics have been changed to protect the privacy of certain individuals.

With Love

Reni Maxwell
Cork Miller
Guy Ron Kimi
Megan and Austen
Sandy
Cyndy Miller
Harold and Joan Lance

Contents

Me and Mom

Prologue

My mother, Lucille Miller, was formally charged with murdering my father on Tuesday, October 13, 1964. By the end of November, the prosecution had announced it was asking for the death penalty, a first involving a woman in the history of San Bernardino County, California, and a rarity in the United States to this day. My mother's case drew intense attention from the press, famous lawyers, and a young reporter, Joan Didion, whose coverage of my family's tragedy would later become "Some Dreamers of the Golden Dream," the first story in *Slouching Towards Bethlehem*, the book that put her on the map.

Joan Didion wanted to interview my mom, but her lawyers advised her to decline, so she did. This was the first of many bad decisions her council imposed on Mom, who was in crisis and traumatized and didn't understand she had a voice in the proceedings.

My mother hated "Some Dreamers of the Golden Dream." She was offended by Didion's description of Alta Loma as "curious and unnatural . . . the fallen eucalyptus bark . . . too dusty, a place for snakes to breed." Alta Loma was a kind of wasteland during the time we lived there, but Bella Vista Road was the exception. Even worse for my mother was the humiliation that Didion included a section of the court transcript of her threats to Arthwell Hayton after he ended their affair the summer of 1964:

> *First, I'm going to go to that dear pastor of yours and tell him a few things. . . . When I do tell him that, you won't be in the Redlands Church anymore. . . . Look, Sonny Boy, if you think your reputation is going to be ruined, your life won't be worth two cents.*

She taught her children to be offended, too, and I hated the essay until I had enough hindsight to see it through new eyes many years later.

My mother believed it was Didion's revenge for turning down the author's request for an interview. The irony is that Didion probably would have found my mother to be a sympathetic character had my mom allowed for the interview. She was tiny, like Didion, weighing less than one hundred pounds at the time of her trial, even though she was pregnant with my little sister, Kimi. She had charm that would have played well in a face-to-face meeting.

Nevertheless, her animus toward the famous author would stay with me well into adulthood. For years, I would be ashamed of Didion's essay. I thought it was cruel, portraying us as a more upscale version of the Joad family of *The Grapes of Wrath*, having moved to California to find the Golden Dream. It wouldn't be until many years later that I would come to terms with just how accurate Didion's portrayal really was.

CHAPTER 1:

Bella Vista Road

In the spring of 1964, we moved to Bella Vista Road, pushed up against the tundra and foothills shielding Mount Baldy, the last public street below King Ranch. Mount Baldy rose above the rolling hills of hard dirt and weed, the foothills of Alta Loma in the arid San Bernardino Valley. Ours was considered the fancy street. There was a lot to do in the foothills: riding, hiking behind our house, catching nonvenomous snakes, helping neighbors save their citrus groves when cold and ice threatened them.

All the homes on our street had been privately built. Although ours was the newest house, it certainly wasn't the nicest. Even so, the truth was that we really couldn't afford it. My mother had forged my father's name on the loan documents. Too depressed and worn out to fight her, he'd let it go, resigning himself to a mortgage payment that, along with everything else, overwhelmed him.

Dirt clods and gravel made up our front and back yards. Our house melted into the brownish dryness surrounding it, looking as though it were an old wreck about to be torn down rather than a newly built house. It seemed to me we had ruined the neighborhood.

We were also a long way from anywhere. Carnelian, the street connecting us to Foothill Boulevard and to civilization, shot north and south for what seemed like miles. Our house stood out for what it didn't have—a lawn, a second story, the kind of trimmings that would make you wish it were yours, which is what all the other houses on the street shared. Even our location set us apart. We were the last house before the gully that blocked any driving from the east end to the west end of Bella Vista. Nothing was in front of us except dirt and orange trees, open spaces interrupted with patches of groves.

My two younger brothers and I saw something comical, even embarrassing, about living on Bella Vista. We didn't fit the neighborhood. We had the pedigree, but some flaw kept us apart. That we'd barely made it up there was obvious. Guy and Ron and I were aware of this and laughed at what a dump our house looked like compared to our neighbors'.

I never felt at home in that unfinished, empty house—empty of furniture, empty of curtains, empty of love and joy but full of anger and despair—an unbearable darkness of being for me but especially for my parents. The house was my mother's dream, not my father's, although during her trial, her friends' testimony contradicted this claim.

I was fourteen, aware of my mother's affair, aware that my father's tears when he drove me to school each morning were the tears of a cuckold: too depressed, too angry, too helpless to change the truth. Tears ran down my face, too, whenever I furtively watched tears running below my dad's black-framed sunglasses, down his cheeks, as we rumbled down Carnelian in our new black Volkswagen. We never spoke.

I hated her then.

CHAPTER 2:

Tension

Years of disconnect stretched between my parents. For my father, it was unhappiness because he hated his profession—dentistry—and the pressure from his wife to make more money. For my mother, it was living with a cold and depressed man, her starvation for love and affection and need for status. It would take many years, looking back on the shadows of unhappiness in our incomplete home, before I would understand the grief that laid the groundwork for what was coming.

My parents didn't shout at each other. The tension on my mother's side was my father's complete lack of affection—not even a "honey" or "sweetie," never a compliment, never an appreciation, and certainly never a kiss or an arm around her, the gestures of love she craved. He was mostly depressed, and sick with headaches. He missed a lot of work. He couldn't give her what she needed. They mostly didn't speak to each other. It was cold comfort for all of us, but especially them.

When I think about my parents, I think of Nathaniel Hawthorne's *The Scarlet Letter,* a story of what happens when a cold man marries a passionate woman. Roger

Chillingworth marries Hester, a much younger woman, expecting her warmth to alleviate his coldness. When he sends her ahead to Boston, she falls in love with another man. Everyone suffers because what has been done can't be undone.

Before moving to Bella Vista Road, we had lived a nomadic life in houses we didn't own. My dad, Gordon Miller, who went by Cork, was an unhappy dentist who would rather have been a pilot or a doctor. His brooding presence contrasted that of my mother's restless personality. She was bored, longing for the better things in life. Their seething anger was palpable. Guy, Ron, and I often were bit players in their domestic drama. Helpless to defend ourselves from the anger and sometimes brutal behavior from our parents, we took it out on each other—fistfights, pounding each other to the ground. One night, I locked Guy out of the house when my parents were gone. For hours he ran around from door to door and window to window, knife clenched in his hand.

Knowing what would happen to us if I told my parents, I never said a word about that night.

All Guy, Ron, and I wanted was physical attention that didn't include belts. All I had to do to stop the escalation of Guy's fury was love him, talk to him with kindness, but I didn't know how to do that. The idea didn't even occur to me.

Nothing was ever cozy and safe on Bella Vista.

CHAPTER 3:

The Burning Car

I did not witness the events of October 7, 1964. What I would come to know of them came from my mother's version later that morning and transcripts from her trial.

This was her version: As my brothers and I slept that night, four months after we'd moved into our new house, my father asked my mother to make him a cup of hot chocolate. She told him that if she did, she wouldn't have enough milk for us kids to have cereal in the morning. There was a store not very far away, but she didn't want to drive the several miles by herself at night to get the milk. She was afraid of the dark; also, she had poor eyesight, and the only prescription glasses she wore were sunglasses, which did little to help her night vision. Glasses were not fashionable in those days, so vanity might have been her reason. She always made fun of herself for wearing those sunglasses at night instead of just buying regular glasses, but she never did anything about it.

Though my father was huddled in a blanket on the couch, feeling sick as usual, he offered to go with her to the store.

She drove while my father, wrapped in the blanket, curled up on the passenger side. He gave her his wallet, which she placed on her lap, then he promptly fell asleep. After checking to make sure the door on my father's side was locked—he was leaning on it, and she was afraid he might fall out—she carefully backed down our steep driveway.

Woody's, the closest market, was about five miles away and was closed by the time they arrived. The lights were still on, and since my mother knew the manager, she banged on the glass door, but no one appeared.

Mayfair, a twenty-four-hour market, was another two or three miles down the road. With my father still asleep, with his wallet lying in her lap, my mother drove there, walked inside, and bought a half gallon of milk. Then she began the trek back home, turning north off Foothill Boulevard onto Sapphire, then right onto Banyan and Carnelian, which was not her usual route to our house. Given my mother's fear of the dark, going that way was an unusual choice. Most of the streets near our house had lights, but Banyan did not. It was pitch black. This became an issue during her trial—why had she gone that way, when normally she never did?

According to my mother, our Volkswagen suddenly lurched to the right onto the berm separating Banyan Street from the orange groves running parallel to it. At the same time, the back seats burst into flames. Terrified, flames singeing her hair, my mother jumped out of the car.

When she turned around, she realized to her horror that flames were consuming my father, who remained slumped against the car door, the blanket wrapped around him melting. She ran to open his door, but when she grabbed the door handle, it radiated so much heat that it burned her hand. She had forgotten she had locked it to keep him safe; now he was trapped in a flaming car.

My mother didn't give up trying to get him out. She ran over the berm into the first row of orange trees searching for something, thinking in her panic she needed to break a window and find a thick branch to push him out of the car. Not knowing what she was doing, she threw a rock barely capable of shattering ordinary glass, much less smashing a thick windshield.

Then my mother remembered a woman who lived in the orange grove and she began running toward what she believed was Carnelian, screaming, "Somebody help me! My husband is burning!" She saw a car ascending a street in the distance, but it was too far away to hear her cries. Just then, she thought it was taking too long to reach Carnelian. Believing she must be running in the wrong direction, she turned around and began running the wrong direction. As she approached our burning car, she witnessed my father's blackened figure leaning against the passenger window of our Volkswagen. Sobbing, she kept running.

Finally, she came to a house and pounded on the door. The woman who answered found my mother incoherent, begging for help, trying to choke out what had just happened. Mrs. Swenson, the woman who answered the door, pulled my mom inside, sat her on the couch, and used her kitchen phone to call the local sheriff's office. She then asked my mom if she wanted her to call anyone. My mother asked her to call Harold Lance, a friend from church.

This became the first of my mother's actions that would be scrutinized later. She thought she was calling a friend who happened to be a lawyer. Investigators believed she called a lawyer who happened to be a friend. While Mrs. Swenson and my mom waited for Harold Lance to arrive, they sat on the couch; my mom rambled on, mentioning what a tough year it had been for our family. Mrs. Swenson smelled burnt hair and noticed a scorched white scarf my mother held. Although my mother's face and hands were smudged and her clothes rumpled, Mrs. Swenson did not see any other dirt or disarray in her appearance.

When Harold Lance arrived, my mom and Mrs. Swenson met him outside. Mom ran up to Harold crying, "My God, it's terrible, Harold. Cork's dead. He's all burned."

Harold said he wanted to return to the accident, but my mom could not initially remember the name of the street the car was on. The Alta Loma Fire Department received a "fire call" from Mrs. Swenson. Because the chief had not been told where the car was, he ended up at the Swenson house just as Harold Lance and my mom were backing out of the driveway, in Harold's silver Porsche, to return to Banyan Street. The chief walked to the passenger side of the car, and Harold introduced himself as a lawyer.

I have always wondered what might have happened if he'd simply introduced himself as a family friend.

Both parties drove to Banyan, the chief following the silver Porsche. When they found the car, it was still burning. My father's charred remains were slumped against the window, a blackened skeleton, about to disintegrate into a heap of ashes. This image would remain imprinted on my brain because one of my brothers later acquired a detective magazine that included a sensationalized version of what happened that night, including a photograph of my father slumped against the window burnt so badly that he was unrecognizable.

Around 2:00 a.m. the morning of October 8, Harold left the scene with my mother to pick up his wife, Joan. When they returned later, three detectives were still there, one of them a homicide detective from the San Bernardino County Sheriff's Department.

Harold, a personal injury attorney, immediately understood the implications of their presence. From an investigator's perspective, only a woman with murder on her mind would have failed to crawl through flames to save her unconscious and burning husband, the father of her children. Harold Lance continued to survey the scene while my mom and

Joan shivered in the shadows. He called his brother, Bud, a criminal attorney, and asked him to drive over to meet him.

When Bud arrived, he and Harold stood off to the side watching how the sheriff's department was investigating. They knew that my mother would be suspected of foul play. It was clear the cops were getting ideas. The investigating team began muscling the lawyers out of the picture, unwilling to give them any information about their inspection. There were things the cops couldn't make sense of, however. They didn't like the position of the car in relation to the embankment at the side of the road. They wondered why the Volkswagen's parking lights were on. How had the car burst into flames when the gasoline tank wasn't ruptured? Why hadn't my father sprung from the car? When the police found an empty, blackened gas can lying on its side in the back seat, Harold whispered to his wife, "Get Lucille out of here. Take her back up to the house." Harold remained at the scene.

By early morning, my father's body had been removed from the car. The darkness drifted away, leaving the coolness of dawn. Harold Lance stood at the scene of the accident, pale and exhausted. The whole thing seemed less spectacular as daylight slowly unveiled the roof of a house here and there, orange groves neatly ordered, stretching away from the sides of the road, the expanse of gray sky dulling the impact of the wreckage of a little black car.

At around six in the morning, Deputy Barnett arrived with the coroner. They wanted to question my mom, who was at home. Harold's brother, Bud Lance, also refused Barnett's request to speak with her, telling him that my mom was in no condition to answer questions.

"We're not going to await her convenience," Barnett responded. "We'll question her even if we have to arrest her."

But they did not leave to arrest her just then.

That came later.

CHAPTER 4:

Daddy's Dead

When I woke up the morning of October 8, something felt wrong. The family room light was on, which scared me because my brothers and I were always up before my parents. I ran back to my bedroom to look out a curtainless window facing the top of our driveway. Where our Volkswagen should have been stood a police car. The house was quiet except for the sound of crushing gravel under the black boots of the police milling around outside. An unfamiliar black pouch, smaller than a briefcase, sat on the kitchen counter. I guessed it was somebody's purse, but whose?

Panicked, I ran to my parents' bedroom. In the middle of their bed, my mom lay curled into a ball wearing her white cotton nightgown. She looked up when she heard me come in.

Immediately, I knew that my father was dead. "Did he kill himself?" I asked.

"No," Mom said, "it was an accident."

"What are the police doing here?" I whispered.

"They come when there's an accident," she replied.

"Why?" I pressed.

"Our car caught on fire."

Her voice flat, sounding dead herself, she tried to explain what had happened. I stood paralyzed, not crying, relieved. It was done, over. My father had threatened to kill himself by driving off a cliff or some other kind of accident that would leave his family with life insurance. It had not been that many nights earlier, during a conflict with my father, that my mother had screamed, "Debbie, grab the car keys and lock yourself in your room!" This was why finding the light on in our family room had scared me. My father stumbled around sometimes, like the time I'd witnessed him trying to take the step up from our living room to the foyer only to crash into a small, hanging crystal lamp. His terrible headaches that kept him home from work made my mom furious. She did a good job of protecting us from all his threats of suicide; I later learned this began early in their fifteen-year marriage.

I remained standing in the silence until my mother told me to "go get the boys." My brothers were still asleep, their little crew-cut heads resting on their pillows, cowboy pajamas peeking out in various places from under the covers. I woke them up but didn't tell them what had happened; even so, they knew something wasn't right. Like I had, they stood at the end of my parents' bed. No one offered comfort to anyone. Guy was eleven, Ron nine. Guy and I started to cry, but Ron ran into the closet because he couldn't cry. Deciding something was wrong with him, he locked himself inside and didn't come out for some time.

At some point, my mother knew she needed help managing the chaos, so she called Sandy, who had been our babysitter since she was sixteen and had come at one point to live with us because of troubles in her own family. She was now twenty-three and in medical school. Sandy didn't waste any time. She jumped in her red 1951 MG and hopped onto the 10 Freeway. It was early enough that the air was still chilly as

Sandy downshifted to make the climb up Carnelian to Bella Vista Road, her MG chugging noisily, her short blond hair blowing in the wind because she always kept the tan canvas top buttoned down to the back of the car.

Within an hour, I heard her engine strain to reach the top of our steep driveway when she arrived. I felt both relief and jealousy at her presence. I loved Sandy, but she had the relationship I wished I could have with my mother. They had such good times together and left me out. Laughing hysterically, they sometimes chased each other around our house. I was in the car once with them when my mom decided to stop at the market to buy two lemon pies. Sandy and Mom told me to wait in the car. This was a common mandate with them—to stay where I was, to not come with them, join them. In short, don't try to be part of our fun. This made me hate Sandy.

When Sandy and Mom emerged from the market, Sandy proceeded to set the pies in the trunk at the same time my mother revved the accelerator. Sandy's face smashed right into the pies, just as my mother intended. Laughing, Sandy cried, "Lucille, how could you do that?" Nobody noticed I was even there. I wanted to cry but sat silently in the back seat.

My mother remained secluded in her bedroom. Ron, Guy, and I didn't know what to do with ourselves. Sandy would comfort us, but there was only so much she could do. We just stood at the end of the bed. My mother would want Sandy, not my brothers, not me. She didn't suspect she was going to be arrested, but she had no control over the sequence of events that was already unfolding that would lead to our lives being upended forever.

Later that morning, Joan Lance arrived and volunteered to take us to her house. The black pouch on the counter turned out to be hers. My brothers and I were stunned, cried, and begged not to leave, but our pleading fell on deaf ears. Suddenly, without explanation, we were being ushered out as fast as possible, shepherded into a metallic-green station wagon.

No one told us what was going on. We were unaware that the situation was developing fast, that the adults around us felt an urgency to remove us from the specter of what was to come. We did not know that it would be a long time before we'd see our mother again.

Later I found out that Sandy tried to console my mother after we left with Joan Lance. She was sobbing and rocking herself, her arms hugging her body as she sat in the middle of her bed. "My children don't have a father," she wept. "There's nothing left of him, nothing for the casket."

Sandy described her as "hysterical." Her only concern was that her children didn't have a father, not even the remains of one. According to Sandy, a woman guilty of murdering her husband wouldn't have gone on like that. Sandy would be one of the few people who would forever maintain my mother's innocence.

Sandy grew so concerned about my mother that she called our family physician, Dr. Mortensen. Dr. Mortensen had been tending my family for years. Tall and bulky, light hair combed to the side, he was a big and gentle man. He strolled to the bed where my mother sat. His firm but soft-spoken bedside manner relaxed her a bit. He was able to get her to lie prone. Dr. Mortensen intravenously gave her Nembutal, a strong sedative and truth serum, and she slipped into a sound sleep.

With Mom gone under, Dr. Mortensen and Sandy whispered about the accident. He promised he'd check on her later, then left.

Two other friends arrived soon afterward to keep watch over my mother. They knew what she did not—that it was only a matter of time before the police arrived to take her away.

CHAPTER 5:

The Arrest

It was in the early afternoon, October 8, and still gray outside when Deputy Sheriff's Detectives Paterson, Karr, and Callahan arrived at our house.

As Sandy remembered years later, the house was quiet and its occupants nervous. Harold Lance had sent his private detective—Don Odle, a big, bulky guy—to our house to protect my mother if the cops tried anything funny. Everyone was expecting something bad to happen.

Sandy was with my mother in the bedroom when she heard muffled voices in the foyer. Mom looked pale and fragile, her long, thin limbs folded into each other, her breathing steady, her thin lips slanting down at the corners, slightly parted. Sandy understood but didn't want to accept what was about to happen.

Don Odle opened our front door, and although they had no warrant, the three deputy sheriff's detectives pushed themselves into our foyer. Odle went to the bedroom to announce the cops had arrived. The next thing Sandy and my mom saw were detectives standing at the bedroom door, one of them using his foot to push it all the way open.

Standing at the foot of the bed, they made it clear they were there to take my mother away. It made Sandy sick to have to wake her, but there was nothing she could do.

Waking my mother was not easy. The doctor's injection was meant to keep her asleep until the next morning. When my mother came to and realized what was happening, she began to cry.

"You are under arrest," one of the officers said.

Mom sat on the side of the bed slumped over, her elbows on her knees, her hands cupping her face. She was sobbing and too unsteady to stand up. Sandy dressed her with one hand and propped her up with the other, trying to get her to stand, trying to help her step into her panties. When Mom asked for a few minutes, one of the detectives replied, "We'll give you five. If you don't hurry up, we'll take you as you are."

What happened next could have been a chase scene in a movie. My mother's lawyers, the brothers Harold and Bud Lance, were braced for the possibility that the officers would try to secrete my mother away. The Lances had decided that their man Odle would park at the end of the driveway and wait at our house for the police. Bud parked on Carnelian, ready to follow the police to wherever they planned to take Mom.

The police escorted my mother in handcuffs out the door as Odle and Sandy followed, grabbing Mom's purse, which police promptly searched. Odle first asked if he could come with them, to which the officers replied, "No, we cannot take you." Odle then explained he wanted to follow them to the sheriff's office. "You are a free citizen," they told him. "You can do what you want."

With Mom handcuffed in the back seat, the deputies backed down the driveway and sped off as Sandy and Odle dashed to his car. Odle had called Bud earlier to inform him of what was going down on Bella Vista Road. Bud wanted to be with Mom when the cops questioned her, so he was already idling his black Porsche on Carnelian. He saw the patrol cars racing past him and pulled out behind them. The cops accelerated when they saw Bud's Porsche behind them. Bud accelerated, too.

Suddenly, a patrol car appeared out of nowhere, sirens screaming and red lights flashing behind Bud. He pulled over. The officer casually stepped out of his car, sauntered over to Bud's car, and told him to get out. Bud stood by the side of the road watching the officer waste time circling his car as if in search of some serious offense. Next the officer put Bud through a sobriety test, making him walk the line. Taking up even more time, he asked Bud question after question but never issued him a citation or arrested him.

Meanwhile, another patrol car had stopped Don Odle and Sandy. Same scenario: The officer leisurely walked around Odle's car, asked him questions, submitted Odle and Sandy to sobriety tests, and took up precious minutes to put distance between Odle and Sandy and the car transporting my mother. No citations were issued.

So no one was surprised that my mother wasn't at the sheriff's station where the officers had claimed she was being taken for questioning.

Harold and Bud desperately phoned around, trying to discover which police station was holding my mother. It took hours to figure out where the police were detaining her.

By the time they did, it was too late.

CHAPTER 6:

Interrogation

Drugged and exhausted, my mother faced questioning without representation. Under these circumstances, she did the worst thing possible. She waived her right to an attorney and babbled on to Sergeant William Paterson. Under the influence of Nembutal, she talked loosely, saying stupid things like, "I have always been basically quite an honest person," and babble such as, "I can put a hat in the cupboard and say it cost $10 less, but basically I've always kind of just lived my life the way I wanted to, and if you don't like it you can take off."

She thought they believed her silly woman routine—one who tells white lies to her husband, whose independence reached no further than shopping a little more than she should and fibbing about it. My mother was a smart woman, but naive. She saw herself as charming and savvy in the ways of the world with an understanding of human nature. She also was a sucker when complimented. She was much easier to figure out than she realized and way more easily manipulated than she could have ever imagined. These were fatal flaws that would get her into trouble for the rest of her life. The open and personable relationship she believed she was intentionally developing with the police was actually their game, not hers. They sat back and let her ramble, laughing with her and encouraging her to chatter on.

By the time her attorneys found her in the San Bernardino County jail late at night on October 8, she had blabbed away her freedom. When the interrogation ended, Mom stood up believing that now that she had told her interrogators the truth, she was free to go home. Instead, they clapped handcuffs on her wrists.

After that disastrous interrogation, everything tilted toward the prosecution. As the case progressed, the prosecution kept the press advised of developments, while the defense refused to talk to the media, yet another mistake her lawyers made. San Bernardino County Sheriff Frank Bland leaked information to Jack Hartsfield of the *San Bernardino Sun-Telegram*. Because the information going to the newspapers came from the prosecution, and because Harold and Bud Lance inexplicably refused to talk to the press, and because detectives refused to notify the Lances if they were going to continue to interrogate her, everything continued to go south.

When Harold and Bud found my mother sobbing and in handcuffs, they knew the police had taken advantage of her condition and naivete. They also knew she couldn't keep her mouth shut. So nine attorneys kept a twenty-four-hour vigil outside her jail cell, including friends and colleagues of Harold and Bud who did this for free, according to court transcripts.

During this time, other detectives fanned out to question family, friends, and my father's office nurse, who revealed a key indiscretion—that my mother was having an affair—and a motive emerged.

My mother's fate was clear. She was headed for an indictment for murdering her husband.

CHAPTER 7:

Losing Everything

During Mom's time in jail, which was from October 8, 1964, until her conviction on March 5, 1965, my brothers and I were at the Lances' and had no idea what was going on. Nor did we know anything about the Lances except that they were friends of my parents' and we attended the same church. Harold seemed stern. Joan, with her high cheekbones and Nordic fair skin and blond hair, was a beauty. Their three children were younger than my brothers and me. Joan dressed her two daughters like the little girls on the cover of *McCall's* magazine. They seemed like the perfect family, especially compared to mine.

The day my mother was interrogated, my brothers sat with the two youngest Lance kids, Jimmy and Julia, on the family room floor's braided rug, watching television. Karen Lance, the oldest of the three Lance children, curled up with me in an oversize chair. I was distracted, trying to listen to the whispered conversations Joan Lance was having on the phone. I was angry because I felt I had a right to know everything that was going on, one more time left out. Then and there in my fourteen-year-old ignorance, I blamed the Lances for everything, believing they were the reason we weren't home.

Soon, Noreen, a family friend and a physical education teacher at Chaffey High School, arrived at the Lances' and asked me if I would like to take a ride with her and drive the car. This wasn't the first time I'd driven her metallic-blue Pontiac with white leather interior down Carnelian from our house, across 19th Street to Sapphire, heading north again to Hillside and across again to Carnelian, back up to our street, Bella Vista, maybe a four-mile square. While I drove, she kept the atmosphere light until we returned to the Lances' house. She directed me to pull to the curb and turn off the engine. Silence. I knew something sad was about to happen. The feeling of joy from driving turned to alarm.

Noreen told me my mother had been arrested.

My reaction to this news came from my dread and my hope, two states of mind very familiar to me and which I'd lived with for many years already.

"Will she be home tonight?" I asked.

"No, I don't think so, Debbie," Noreen replied. She explained that the police needed to ask my mom some questions.

I started to cry. There was nothing more to say.

We would never live as a family again.

About a week after my mother's arrest, my father's funeral was held. My mother's lead attorney, Edward P. Foley, had pleaded with Superior Judge John W. Kerrigan that she be allowed to attend her husband's funeral with her children. But by then the toxicology report on my father had revealed that he had been heavily drugged at the time of his death. The autopsy confirmed he had been alive but unconscious when the car burned. It was all over the media, the belief that my mother had drugged him and burned him to death.

Assistant District Attorney Don A. Turner argued that she should not be allowed to attend the funeral to avoid a "Ruby–Oswald incident," implying that someone might show up and shoot my mother like Jack Ruby had shot and killed Lee Harvey Oswald after Oswald had been arrested for the assassination of President John F. Kennedy. Judge Kerrigan agreed and ruled against my mother to protect her from someone who might "try to take the case into his own hands."

My mother's request to attend the funeral was denied.

CHAPTER 8:

The Alabaster Box

I have little memory of my father's funeral except that it was a media madhouse. Guy, Ron, and I arrived all alone in a limousine and then got ushered through swarms of people, cameras flashing all around us, from the limousine to the funeral hall and back again. We sat in the front pew, stoic, the closed casket containing our father's remains in front of us. We didn't cry. I was in some kind of dream.

My mother owned a small alabaster jewel box that sat on her bathroom counter, whiter than the fake marble countertop. The day she left us, it disappeared. But there it stood, although this one was much larger. It must have been a gift from her, a final loving gesture to her husband. My father's casket, the giant alabaster box, stood regally on a platform with a celestial light shining on it.

My body sat in the pew, but my spirit was not with it; it floated of its own accord up to the casket. I wrapped my arms around the coffin as best I could. It felt cold but looked beautiful and peaceful. I felt happy because the heavens were shining on my daddy. He was protected inside this precious box. I didn't cry because I knew he was happier now in God's kingdom.

I wanted to stay under that soft light. I felt safe and secure in my illusion of clinging to that sarcophagus. In my mind, my brothers' spirits soon joined me. Dr. Miller's children were being blessed with the spirit, the soft light purifying and protecting them, wrapping itself around them, an invisible armor shielding them from what was to come, not preventing the pain and sorrow to follow but promising them redemption in the faraway future. As our earthly bodies walked into the chaos of reality, the cameras flashed, people pressed forward.

All I remember is having been given the grace to feel my daddy's presence one last time.

CHAPTER 9:

From the Beginning

My mother was born in Winnipeg, Canada, on January 17, 1930, the only child of Lily and Gordon Maxwell, teachers and strict Seventh-day Adventists. When my mother was in her late teens, her parents took jobs in Walla Walla, Washington, a typical Adventist community that included a church grade school, high school, and college. My grandfather became the high school principal, and my grandmother, nicknamed Tubby, was head of the college's Music Conservatory. My mother entered Walla Walla College as a freshman to get what she called her "MRS degree," a mindset that later translated to her not encouraging me to get good grades.

My father, the third child of Hazel and Guy Miller, also came from a strict Adventist family who lived in Walla Walla. He had an older sister, Genevera, and an older brother, Doug; Genevera was about eleven years older than my dad and adored her baby brother. They were an affluent family who owned hardware stores.

My father was not raised with hugs and affection. He became a dentist even though he had no interest in it; he had chosen this profession because his brother and brother-in-law were dentists. He practiced dentistry in Walla Walla, as did his older brother, Doug, and his brother-in-law, Tom Thompson. Young and single, he was a ladies' man. He would drive around town in his red convertible, the guy to catch, the most desired bachelor, and often cruised around the Walla Walla college campus trolling coeds.

One day in 1949, my mother caught his eye. What called his attention to her was how outgoing she appeared strolling around with her group of friends. My mother enjoyed being the center of attention and understood how to capture it; she was not just pretty—fine features, dark hair styled in a short-feathered flip—she was gregarious, rebellious, exciting. After inquiring about who she was, he sent her two dozen red roses. They were married three months later on April 10, 1949.

Many years later, an interviewer asked my mom when she realized her marriage was in jeopardy. Laughing, she replied, "My marriage was in jeopardy as soon as I said 'I do.'"

During World War II and immediately after, the army established accelerated dental programs intended for the best and the brightest. My father was recruited to participate in the dental program at the University of Oregon's Dental College. He was twenty-one when he graduated and automatically became a lieutenant. Just before the Korean conflict, the newlyweds were ordered to Guam, and later Japan.

I was born in Guam, and the trouble began during those overseas years. The climate of their marriage was full of clouds and storms and very little sunshine from early on.

When I was a teenager, my mother told me stories about life in Guam and in Japan. Guam, hot and humid, left you feeling sweaty and sticky. Insects such as giant cockroaches required that the legs of my crib stand in pails of water to keep them from getting to me. My father would stand over my crib and coo, his made-up language of affection. "You're the Tikums of the Tikums of the Dirty Mean Stuff," he'd say, but mostly he called me "Dirty Means," which translated to "you are my precious baby girl and I love you."

On the other hand, my nineteen-year-old mother witnessed the worst of my father, his coldness and lack of affection, along with flashes of sadism, like the time he swung a dead mouse over her face to wake her up.

This is all I know of Guam, except that my mother hated it. She felt despair and fear about her future with my father. Years later, she lamented not having left right then and taken me back to the States with her. She would cry about these memories, then she would remind herself that had she left, there never would have been a Guy and a Ron.

With the Korean War looming, our little family relocated to Kyoto, Japan, as my father awaited word about whether he would go to war or return home. There, my mother bought translucent porcelain china with gold trim and a beautiful collection of Imari coffee cups and saucers. I grew up with tchotchkes intricately carved from elephant tusks. My father purchased a huge Imari plate, a majestic cloisonné eagle fixed in the center. Yet my mother's stories about what should have been exotic experiences were instead about abuse and fear. According to her, I was a victim of cruelty, too. When I was two, I often would turn my head away when my parents tried to feed me, a typical toddler move. But it made my parents desperate; they sought advice from the family doctor, who recommended spanking. So the new routine to force me to eat was to unlatch the high chair, remove my diaper, and spank me.

In Kyoto, we lived on the American army base. Joyce and Boyson were a couple whose job was to take care of me, washing me outside in a tin washtub, loving and spoiling me in a way I'd never experience again. My mom had lots of pictures of me in that tub, looking up at Joyce and Boyson and smiling broadly. They sobbed when my mother, twenty years old by then, boarded a steamship with her toddler for the United States. My father would remain in Japan a few more months to finish his tour of duty.

The journey home included a typhoon, terrifying my mother because I screamed and vomited so much, she thought I might die. She sobbed. I puked. But we survived and made it back to the States, where we stayed with my mom's parents until Daddy was discharged.

CHAPTER 10:

Stateside

When my father returned to us, we moved to the farthest northwest part of Oregon to the community of Enterprise in one of the valleys in Wallowa County, sometimes referred to as Little Switzerland. It is a beautiful place with snow-tipped mountains, blue glacial lakes, and abundant Douglas firs and pines. Other nearby valleys consisted of cattle ranches and farms and logging industries, which flourished after the bombing of Pearl Harbor, triggered by an increase in construction.

My grandfather owned the only medical building in Enterprise, which sat across the street from the courthouse and next to the library. When we moved there, my father joined his brother, Doug, as the second of two dentists in this small town.

Our first house was green, the last one on the top of a hill. It had a huge picture window in the living room with a clear view of Enterprise's municipal center, consisting of a wooden courthouse built in the middle of the town and a church, both white, surrounded by trees. Guy and Ron were born in this house.

It is winter. Everything is white. I feel the sharp breeze and the smell of pines and furs. My parents drag out our toboggan, pile Guy and me onto it, and zip to the bottom of the hill. As I grow older, I will use my own sled to recklessly slide, screaming at the top of my lungs, to the bottom of the hill.

There are darker memories, too. One afternoon, I scoot down the porch steps to our front lawn when our dog Shep, happy to see me, bounds toward me, jumps up to greet me, and, without meaning to, knocks me down. My parents hear my cries and run to see what happened. I choke out that Shep knocked me down. Out of "love for me," my father gets his shotgun, takes Shep out back, and shoots him. My guilt, my sorrow, and my tears! I understood that something awful happened to Shep and it was my fault.

We soon moved outside Enterprise into a smaller white clapboard house my grandfather owned. That was where Sally came to us in a wooden crate. I was five. Guy was three, and Ron, one. My father knelt down, his arms wrapped around the crate, and gently settled it on our living room floor. Sally stood quivering on her short legs, black and brown, peering through the slats. The name Sally was my dad's pick for our new dachshund, short for salami.

Sally became my father's pride and joy. He nicknamed her "Sal Bitch," which made my mother laugh. Guy, Ron, and I never sat on my father's lap, but Sally curled up to him every night on our couch. She bounced up and down on her stubby little legs when my father came home from work. She was so low to the ground, so long and pointed, so arrogant and possessive of my father. I hated her.

One day, I decided to see how those legs would fare once tossed off our deck. I employed Guy to do my dirty work. He picked Sally up and dropped her off the side of our deck. Sally yelped and yelped and couldn't move. My mother heard her cries of distress and came running. She swooped Sally up in her arms.

I instantly turned in my brother for this crime. He didn't think or didn't know to turn me in as the real culprit. He received a serious spanking. Nothing happened to me. After we rushed her to the vet's office, we learned that all four of Sally's legs were severely sprained. The minute I heard her cry out, I felt guilty. Because of the attention my father showered on Sally rather than me, I remained Sally's enemy.

My father and his brother occupied two offices in my grandfather's medical building. Our family physician, Dr. Ham, occupied the office at the end of the foyer. One of the doctor's sons, Bruce Ham, was a year older than me. We attended the two-room Adventist school not far from my grandfather's building, where we spent our after-school hours until we drove home with our families.

One afternoon on our way to our parents' office, Bruce Ham and I were wearing our snowsuits and gloves as we tramped down the hill of our school into a huge snow-filled gulley. We stopped and built a kind of cave igloo, big enough for one of us to crawl into. It got dark and we got colder, so we abandoned our snow cave and literally tumbled and laughed our way down to town.

Soaking in the warmth of the building, we stamped the snow off our boots, climbed out of our snowsuits, and peeled off our gloves before we climbed down the stairs in our snow boots to the bright lights and warmth of the building's basement. Waiting for us was a refrigerator stocked with soda and a carrom table, a small square board with rounded edges and net pockets (Seventh-day Adventists consider pool sinful, and carrom is a substitute). We opened the refrigerator for a soda. My favorite was orange soda.

Then we shuffled, sodas in hand, to the carrom table or to play Rook. (Adventists also aren't allowed to play cards, but Rook is okay. These are considered Christian cards, marketed to take the place of a standard deck of cards, which are associated with gambling. Rook cards have colored numbers called suits. It's a points game.)

Because the basement was unfinished, it had lots of tunnels to explore, our favorite activity. The deeper we ventured, the darker it got and the scarier, too, which was the whole point.

Once my father was no longer in the army, he began hating dentistry even more. When in the service, he was not responsible for anything but his work. He liked being a lieutenant and having housing and other amenities provided for him. He liked not having pressure. He should have stayed in the military.

He dreamed of becoming a commercial pilot, in the cockpit, away from everyone else. He liked gliding above the earth and feeling the immensity of the universe, safely encapsulated in a metal tube, surrounded by openness. It made him feel free, something that standing on solid ground didn't give him. He instead settled for applying to the Adventist Medical Center in Loma Linda, California, to become a doctor and escape dentistry. That's why we moved, though he never ended up attending medical school. I don't know why. I guess arriving in California with three kids, a bossy dachshund, and an impatient wife forced him to buy a dental practice, and he allowed his dream of being a pilot or a physician to fade. But not without consequences to his well-being.

Before our move, my parents made a trip to California, which meant I stayed with my mother's parents in Portland. My grandmother Tubby enrolled me in first grade.

One day, the teacher asked each student what they wanted to be when they grew up. Everyone seemed to have this figured out. When it was their turn, each student easily replied that they wanted to be a nurse or a fireman or another profession, noteworthy ambitions applauded by all.

I was dreading my turn because I had no idea what I wanted to be. I had never thought about it. I was in the middle of searching my mind when the teacher called on me.

"I want to be a beautician!" I blurted out.

The room went silent. I instantly understood that I had picked a less worthy future than the other first-graders. I felt humiliated. The silence in the room echoed its disapproval. At that moment, I floated outside of my body. I was embarrassed and ashamed.

CHAPTER 11:

California

Finally, my parents returned to Oregon to reclaim their children, and we made our way to California in 1958 stuffed in a red Pontiac with a white leather interior. I like to believe we rolled into Upland, California, in our Pontiac on the legendary Route 66. I know we did pull into a Travelodge motel, the one with a bear hugging the marquee. It was pink, which was already one of my favorite colors, and it had a swimming pool. This was our camp until my parents found a house to rent, which only took a couple of days.

We all stayed in the same room. My brothers and I spent our days hanging out at the pool and splashing around in it. We were vegetarians, and Mom would call us up to the room and make tomato sandwiches on Wonder Bread along with a side of cottage cheese and vegetarian beans. These were happy days for our family. It was a rebirth, my parents starting over, falling in love with each other again and with their children. Often, we ate dinner at a coffee shop, ordering grilled cheese sandwiches and french fries.

It was a lovely time that was about to come to an abrupt end.

We moved from the Travelodge into a tract house in Upland, similar to the Levittown tract homes William Levitt and his sons built on Long Island and elsewhere after World War II. This memory is more a feeling, forever dark. Anger filled that house, and it landed on me. I didn't comprehend what must have happened when we arrived, that my father's medical school plans fell through. The reason for moving to California had vanished.

I was about to restart first grade again at a new school. I was terrified at the thought of attending yet another school. I understood at age seven that everyone at my new school would have formed their friendships, and I believed I would not be able to find a friend. My mother stepped up. She treated the situation gently, assuring me I would fit in and make friends. She held my hand as we walked into the school. Seventh-day Adventist schools were always tiny, often built with only two classrooms. Grades one through four were in one room, and grades five through eight in the other. The little white clapboard school in Ontario, California, was no different.

When we reached the door of Mrs. Abbot's classroom, my mother knocked and a blue-haired lady stepped out to meet us. My mother introduced me and requested that Mrs. Abbot introduce me to the most popular girl in the class. Mrs. Abbot said she knew the perfect girl. She returned with Terry Hayton, who reached for my hand and washed away my fears.

Terry was taller and fleshier than me. I saw myself as knobby-kneed and scabby, whereas she was poised and confident. Her hair was blonder, but we both wore our long blond tresses braided tightly at the bottom with bright colored ribbons. Terry wore a brown and yellow print dress her mother had sewn for her, yellow buttons dotting the front. She had a beautiful face, all smiles and softness.

I immediately fell in love with her. She became my best friend.

After the war, processed and canned food arrived in supermarkets. The worst was canned peas. Mothers were thrilled with the convenience, children not so much. My brothers and I were doomed at the dinner table. Compromise of any sort didn't exist. My brothers and I sat at the dinner table, clock ticking as we gagged down our cold, mushy peas.

But there were pleasures in this house, too, the pleasures my body offered me.

I was forbidden to touch my body in this way, of course, given my parents' religious beliefs.

One night, my parents had let me sleep in their bed as a treat. They had just come home from an evening out, and my mother felt my forehead. Finding it was warm and sweaty, she accused me of much nastiness. Fearful, I denied it, but she didn't believe me. She told my father, who pulled me out of bed and whipped my bare bottom black and blue. Guy would tell me many years later that our father would stand them next to each other to see if they had an erection.

I couldn't stop pleasuring myself, so much so that I became public about it, clutching classmates' shoulders to balance myself. I remember standing in the garage thinking how good I felt, understanding that someone might tell on me and I would be whipped, and I'll never forget my little eight-year-old mind decided the release through the pleasure was worth a beating.

Seventh-day Adventism is a religion founded by a prophet, Ellen G. White. My father owned and subscribed to all of her teachings.

In her book *Child Guidance,* she wrote, "Those who have charge of God's property in the souls and bodies of the children formed in His image should erect barriers against the sensual indulgence of the age, which is ruining the physical and moral health of thousands. If many of the crimes of this time were traced to their true cause, it would be seen that they are chargeable to the ignorance of fathers and mothers who are indifferent on this subject."

My brothers and I read little red books of fiction that served to reinforce what happens when you are bad. We also had a beautiful group of leather-bound books, brightly colored Jesus pictures on the covers and more pictured pages inside telling the story of Jesus.

Around this time was when Sandy became our babysitter. We didn't get off to a good start. When my parents arrived home the first night, she reported that I had resisted going to bed. She did not understand the consequences I would suffer for this minor infraction.

By then, I had fallen asleep peacefully, but suddenly, my bedroom light switched on. My father grabbed me out of bed, dragged me half asleep to the bathroom, belt in hand, and whipped me. I was screaming. I tried to get away, but he just pulled me back and whipped me harder and longer. I didn't know what I had done wrong. Sandy and my mom stood in the living room listening to my screams. No one told him to stop. No one saved me. I was eight years old. I thought he was going to beat me to death.

I returned to my bed sobbing, welts on my legs and butt, everything turning black and blue. My mother came into my bedroom, lifted me out of bed, and walked me to the living room, where my father sat on the couch watching television.

She sat me down beside him. This was to prove he loved me even though he had thrashed me. He ignored me.

I felt humiliated and angry. If I'd dared, I would have pulled back from her, run back to my bed, and hidden under the covers.

Many years later, Sandy told me that no matter how naughty I had been, after witnessing what my father would do to his eight-year-old daughter, she never told my parents again.

Our next move was to a house on Cypress Avenue in Ontario. I was ten. I spent a lot of my time getting sick and was always treated like a queen during these illnesses. My mother would pack me up in blankets, move me to the living room couch, and let me watch *As the World Turns*. She also planned my meals around whatever I wanted, mostly Campbell's tomato soup and grilled cheese sandwiches, pimento olives or dill pickles on the side. One night, my father came home with an oversize coloring book, a box of sixty-four crayons, and a big brown teddy bear.

This was when Sandy came to live with us, a refugee from an abusive mother.

It happened all at once, with a bang on our front door. When my father opened it, Sandy's mom pushed her way into our house, caught sight of Sandy, bolted toward her, dragged her into our bathroom, locked the door, and began beating her daughter with her fists as Sandy screamed for help. Somehow, my parents talked Sandy's mom down and got her to open the door. Sandy dashed to safety as my father forcefully escorted her mother out of our house.

Sandy ended up sharing my room, not something I wanted. My mom assured me that I had complete control and that Sandy would abide by my rules.

With that power, how could I resist? My rules included no clothes being left around and the bed had to be made the minute Sandy got up, even if she had to go to the bathroom in the middle of the night. My mother did not intervene to stop my behavior. I can only think I acted this way to feel I was in control, where I often had none.

Our last move before Bella Vista was into a house in Ontario on College Way, a cul-de-sac. I always loved this little green cottage, with its huge backyard, several trees worth climbing, and a red concrete patio decked out with a brick grill, including a chimney, which was the cockpit of our ship, the place where the captain, always me, stood lookout for the imaginary enemy. I never could figure out if I was a tomboy or a regular girl in those days. I loved climbing up the brick grill to the chimney and slipping into it, then standing on the ledge inside it. I could easily survey my empire from this height or duck down and hide. I also loved the sweet lavender beauty of my bedroom, the smell of the bluegrass cologne my mother bought for me. Everything I owned was plentiful and beautiful. I was my mother's doll in a dollhouse bedroom.

But beneath that facade was conflict. I spent a lot of time in my bedroom because I was always being punished, which I didn't mind because I loved being alone.

My parents often spent weekends in Las Vegas with their friends, leaving us with Sandy, who would come up from medical school. If we stayed behind, we would take care of Sally. When they returned home, my father would give me his silver dollars; I collected so many silver dollars that he bought me a safe for my stash, which I regularly counted and restacked whenever I was banished to my bedroom.

One time when they returned home, my father immediately called for Sally. Somehow, she had gone missing. He blamed me and was furious. I was panicked to find that dog. Sandy and I spent the afternoon combing the neighborhood calling for Sally. I felt I could never go home again if I couldn't find her.

Finally, as Sandy and I were walking back to our house after our futile search, we heard Sally yapping. She was trapped in a neighbor's driveway because he had shut the gate, not realizing Sally was there. I was furious at that damn dog.

Sally gave me another reason to hate her not long after that. My father walked in the door one evening carrying two baby guinea pigs in a small cage. He built a wonderful roomy home for them, a castle compared to what the pet stores carried. We set it on the brick counter of a fancy outdoor grill we never used for cooking.

Mutt and Jeff were redheads. Jeff had long and silky hair, while Mutt's hair looked like it had been combed every which way and then hair-sprayed. I adored both and took good care of them. I watched them grow, cleaned their cages religiously, fed them, and made sure they always had a bowl of water. Mutt and Jeff loved perching on my shoulders, squeaking happiness and contentment. I would lie on my bed and let them sniff me. Once they were satisfied it was me, they would crawl under my hair. My mother told everyone how much my guinea pigs loved to cuddle in my long hair.

One day, we moved Mutt and Jeff's cage on the patio into the shade. Either the latch on their cage had been left open or Sally was smart enough to unhook the latch with her long nose, but suddenly I heard growling and Mutt and Jeff squeaking as loud as their little lungs allowed. I turned to see that fat old wiener dog's body stuffed halfway through the cage door with Mutt in her mouth as she shook him. Jeff was scrunched back in a corner. I screamed for my mother. Somehow, we got Sally out of that cage. Mutt was mangled and dead. Poor little Jeff had died of a heart attack watching what he must have seen as a huge black beast murder his brother.

I was sobbing, screaming at Sally about how much I hated her. My mother found a shoebox, and while I wept, cradling my dead babies in their little coffin, someone dug a hole in the backyard and we buried them. I was inconsolable. I wanted my family to get rid of that dog.

Trying to ease my grief, my father arrived home that night with three new guinea pigs, Suzet, Babett, and Collett. But while my sorrow was briefly lifted, it wasn't the same. Maybe I didn't have love in my heart to tend to them the way I had Mutt and Jeff, but the new guinea pigs didn't love me. The feeling was mutual.

Throughout our many moves, anger always was there. When we lived on College Way, I picked up the phone at the same time my mother did, and she didn't realize I was listening. My father's receptionist had called to warn my mother that he was coming home to pack his belongings and leave us. My mother and the receptionist knew why this was happening, but I didn't and was terrified.

About an hour later, my father stormed into the house and straight back to their bedroom. Seconds later, with his jockey shorts in one hand and his baby-blue transistor radio in the other, he left the house without a word.

I started to cry. My mother tried to comfort me, assuring me he would come home.

He did, but nothing more was ever said about the incident.

There was some normalcy. My mom taxied her kids to tennis lessons, swimming lessons, and ice-skating lessons like every other mom. When I turned out to be lousy at tennis and hated it, she let me quit.

Piano did not go well. One of my music teachers told her I had a perfect ear. She decided I was a prodigy and turned piano practice and lessons into punishment, telling my piano teachers to report on my progress, setting the time clock along with the metronome when I practiced and otherwise being furious with me all of the time. I rewarded her by never making it through a recital without tons of mistakes and didn't turn out to be very good at playing the piano, much less a prodigy.

Mom played the piano beautifully, her long, polished nails clicking across the keys, while I stood happily beside her singing "Winter Wonderland," "Que Sera, Sera," and my favorite, "Moments to Remember."

CHAPTER 12:

Joyful Times

When my mom wasn't around, Sandy and I had fun. The hilarity began whenever my parents weren't home. Sandy would flip on the radio to rock and roll or slide a forty-five onto our record player, dancing my brothers and me around the living room. My favorites were The Beach Boys and Jan and Dean. Because Seventh-day Adventism forbids dancing, we didn't know how. When my brothers and I started to fall, Sandy held our hands and dragged us around our living room until we all dropped to the floor in a heap, sweaty and laughing. We agreed that if we were to continue dancing with Sandy, my parents couldn't know.

We often visited Sandy at Squires, the restaurant where she worked during the summer, which offered more fun because she was always happy to see us and served us grilled cheese sandwiches with french fries and introduced us to all the waitresses.

The last joyous Christmas we had was December 25, 1963. The following year, my father was dead, my mother was on trial for his murder, my brothers lived in Washington State, and I was left rudderless without any family.

Despite harsh discipline and smoldering anger between my parents, that Christmas was beautiful, just like every other one before it. My mom loved the holidays and made them fantastical. Christmas Eve was my favorite. We celebrated our last Christmas at our house on College Way. My mom ordered a white frosted pine and decorated it with huge red balls, as was her tradition. She set up her porcelain nativity scene around the fireplace and Santa sleighs and other Christmas icons all around the living room. It looked like a storybook picture. Mom also baked dozens of Russian teacakes, little white snowballs made of butter, confectioners' sugar, flour, and walnuts that melted in our mouths. She baked a special kind of oatmeal cookie using rolled dough and red plastic cookie cutters. Guy, Ron, and I used to cut out Santa in his sleigh, reindeer, Santa with his arm up waving, and an angel.

Mom stopped off at the best restaurant in town, the Sycamore Inn, and asked if she could have several of their empty industrial-sized condiment jars. She would use those to store her cookies, beginning with a layer of wax paper, cookies carefully positioned on the paper, more wax paper, more cookies until the jar was full. We made popcorn balls and Bing Crosby sang "White Christmas" and "Silver Bells" on our Christmas collection of thirty-threes. Our house smelled of pine and cinnamon from Christmas candles and baked goods. The bottom of our tree was always packed with Christmas gifts. If you asked for it, you got it; it worked every Christmas at our house.

My mother's parents flew down from Portland, Oregon, to join us. A few years earlier, my grandfather, a talented amateur artist, had given my mother a large oil painting, a crude seascape, green water dashing up against huge brown boulders. She hated it. But this year, just as she had every Christmas since she got it, she pulled the painting out of the closet, just before my grandparents arrived, and mounted it behind our couch.

Once my grandparents arrived, we shopped. Three generations of women—Tubby, Mom, and me—spent an afternoon shopping for Christmas presents at Bullock's in Pasadena. Mother gave me money to buy Christmas presents, and this year would be like every other year before it—soap on a rope for each of my brothers, hankies for my dad, nylons for my mother. My predictability was a family joke. But it's not that I marched straight to the soap or hankie counter. I strolled into Bullock's each Christmas resolved to find new and different gifts. I spent hours wandering through each department, scrutinizing every possibility. Somehow, in the end, time always ran out before my prospects, and I would rush to purchase my old standards, certain that these were everyone's favorites anyway.

We opened our presents on Christmas Eve. My mother made a light supper, then my father played Santa Claus, without the red suit, dispensing gifts to everyone in the room. There were no surprises, but the excitement never waned. After opening our gifts, we munched on cookies and sipped hot chocolate until we were off to bed. Christmas Day was my favorite—scrambling out of bed on Christmas morning to delight in our new toys, the traditional dinner, turkey, stuffing, and homemade pies, lots of family around. Life was good.

Yet the results of tension in our family were noticed. A distant cousin would tell me many years later that she always thought the three of us children were too well-behaved. We knew the drill. We did not chase each other around the house, screaming in delight. We weren't running in and out of the house letting the door bang behind us. We knew not to pester our parents with questions or expect them to stop what they were doing to see the way I had arranged the furniture in my new dollhouse or how my brothers had set up their erector set. Our parents were not available as our audience. They did not want to listen to our noise. No one wanted a whipping on Christmas. So to an outsider we were too quiet, too mannered and reserved. But we didn't know anything else.

That said, I never felt afraid during the Christmas season.

The summer of 1964 would prove to be another last: our family's last trip to a cabin owned by my father's parents, where we summered every year. It was located at the head of Wallowa Lake on the Wallowa River, about thirteen or fourteen miles from Enterprise, Oregon. Once we turned onto the dirt road leading to the cabin, the forest opened up. The cabin included a large living room with a fireplace, a kitchen and a breakfast nook, a wood stove for cooking and baking, and three bedrooms and one indoor bathroom for the adults. The other two bedrooms were separated by a pine divider that didn't reach the ceiling, making it possible for the grandchildren tucked under heavy quilts, at least three to a bed, to whisper to each other.

When we arrived, my grandfather was sitting perfectly still in his lounge chair, a smile creeping across his face as he held out his hand full of peanuts, inviting the squirrels who suspiciously approached his outstretched arm, palm up, to steal the nuts and scamper off. We stood quietly, practically holding our breath as a cautious squirrel slowly made its way to my grandfather's outstretched arm and hand. He didn't hold his hand down to the ground. Rather, he got those silly squirrels to climb up his chair and onto his leg and over to his open palm. It was beautiful and amazing to watch. Not one of us, even when we tried emulating his routine, ever enticed a single squirrel to eat nuts from the palm of our hands. Grandpa Miller was not a warm man, and I don't remember a word he ever said to me, but his magic charmed those squirrels, which in turn charmed us. This was proof to me that there was more to him than I could understand.

All the grandkids played outside all day. We played grocery store, picking tin cans out of the garbage pit and arranging them on the shelves we created from the woodpile. My grandparents also tied a green and yellow hammock between two trees. My cousin Tommy, who seemed so much older than the rest of the cousins, liked to hang out in the hammock, wrapping the canvas around him to create a cocoon and holding on tight as he summoned us to swing him around. He never fell out. When our turns came, we fell instantly to the ground as soon as the hammock turned upside down.

Outside the kitchen was a big green wooden picnic table, where Saturday afternoon potlucks happened following church services. The west fork of the Wallowa River curved around the back of the cabin, the rushing water from a powerhouse above it crashing over mottled boulders. One access to the river from the cabin included steep wooden stairs. The river was dangerous and cold, good for keeping a watermelon cold but not for navigation.

One Saturday after church, we spent the afternoon at the Hams' house. Tommy's family had originally owned this house. It was on Hurricane Creek Road a mile or two from Enterprise and just past the road that led to Wallowa Lake. Feasting on yet another potluck, we then spent the rest of the afternoon having a blast with our cousins and the three Ham boys, the oldest of whom, Leslie, was my unrequited crush. We were free to do whatever we wanted. The house was big with lots of lawn all the way around it. One side of the Ham house was all tall picture windows facing a pond surrounded by willow trees and a rowboat waiting for us on the dock. We could chase each other around the pond, or we could row around it. No swimming, though; the water was filled with plant life and probably snakes.

As the sun set and the Sabbath ended, evening festivities began, first a dinner of leftovers and then lots of popcorn and homemade fudge, which is when I discovered how much I liked the combination of sugar and salt. Since it was a sin to go to a movie theater, the Hams substituted reels of cartoons and Seventh-day Adventist movies projected onto a screen in their living room. My favorite movie, a love story, included a pretty teenager who saw the light of God and who ate beans from a tin plate.

During the first week in August, the Wallowa County fairgrounds opened in Joseph, named in 1880 for Chief Joseph (1840–1904) of the Nez Perce Indians. The fairground included a Ferris wheel and other rides and booths that handed out prizes of teddy bears and other stuffed animals if you could toss a ball into cups or throw a dart at floating balloons.

During the last week in July, Joseph celebrated Chief Joseph Days with rodeos. These two celebrations still happen every summer. My girlfriend Sherry lived in Joseph. After a night at the fair during Chief Joseph Days, we crawled out of bed early and hit the fairgrounds to collect glass pop bottles: 2 cents for small bottles and 5 cents for big ones. We spent our money on candy.

I felt free. Nothing bad happened that summer. I only felt joy.

CHAPTER 13:

Omens 1964

When my father arrived home from work, he never acknowledged my mom. Instead, he plopped on the couch in the family room, took Sally onto his lap, and turned on the news. Because Seventh-day Adventists consider drinking a sin, my mom created her own version of a cocktail for my father. She kept orange sherbet in the freezer with a glass teacup that fit into a brass holder with a handle, her version of a martini glass. She also kept Vernors ginger ale in the refrigerator. When she watched him come in from the garage and walk straight to the couch, she wanted to welcome him home, help him relax. Without a greeting, a kiss, or a hug, she began preparing his refreshment. She removed her cocktail glass and the sherbet from the freezer, poured the ginger ale into the glass teacup, floated the sherbet on top, placed her creation on a fancy saucer carpeted with a paper doily, and served it to my father. He never thanked her or used an affectionate pet name.

My father also had a bizarre way of referring to sex, she told me later. Seeming to think it was funny, in front of their friends, my father would announce when he wanted to go home and make love to his wife, "Let's go home. I want to dip my wick."

The spiral downward for my family began in the spring of 1964. It was around this time that my mother confided in me that she was having an affair with Arthwell Hayton, her best friend's husband who was a prominent attorney in Redlands. Even though my mother was cheating with Arthwell, Elaine Hayton had no idea and confided to my mom when she found a gold bracelet on the front floor of his 1964 Cadillac DeVille. Whether this was my mother's bracelet or another woman's, I never found out.

Arthwell Hayton always gave me the creeps, his year-round salon-produced tan, that unsettling gleam in his eye, a smile that always felt forced and insincere to me. I found him unctuous and didn't trust him—call it a child's intuition. Once their affair began, Mom did not spare her family the details. She confided in me, her fourteen-year-old, and seemed utterly unconcerned about hiding her indiscretions from my father.

His response to her flaunting her affair was to withdraw. He had more headaches and regularly popped pills.

One Saturday before church, I came down the steps of my parents' bedroom into the living room in my red patent shoes and a navy-blue sailor dress with a red and white bib attached to the front. My father sat sullenly on the window seat. He looked at me and said, "You look absolutely stunning, darling, in that dress." I understood immediately that he was mimicking the oily voice of Arthwell Hayton and replied equally insincerely, "Thank you."

My mother had declared she was no longer going to attend church. Thrilled to have my father to myself, I asked if he would come to the Adventist Church near my school. We sat in the balcony, where I pretended he was my boyfriend and hoped that all my friends would think so too. I felt proud singing hymns standing next to this handsome man with the beautiful baritone voice. In the end, however, I chose her over him. I stopped going to church as well. I wanted my mother's approval. I wanted to be like her.

A week later, my father moved into a spare bedroom at a friend's house. He came home every night for dinner, a rather awkward arrangement because no one knew what to say. He didn't arrive to hug his children or give us assurances. My parents didn't try to make nice for us. Most nights I was filled with anxiety. I picked at my food. I wanted him to leave. This was worse than living with his moodiness. Within a week, he moved back home.

A few days later, I was standing at the foot of my mother's bed when she told me, "Daddy and I are going to get a divorce."

"I'm going to live with him," I said. Maybe I thought I could change him, make him happier.

Her face turned mean. "Go ahead. You'll soon feel what it's like to live with him." My mother's response delivered the impact she'd intended. She made me afraid.

Sally was an old lady by the time we lived on Bella Vista Road, mostly limping around. We had acquired two other dogs over time, a yappy little poodle named Coquette and Missy, our new Samoyed puppy. My father paid no attention to them. Sally remained his queen. With our new furry snowball Missy to love, I ignored Sally. Coquette, unable to compete with a firmly established old lady or a new woolly puppy, found a new family down the street to love her and moved out.

It was after a weekend outing in September 1964 when we came home, as usual, my father straining the Thunderbird to reach the top of the driveway. It was cloudy outside, and my father got out of the car to open the garage door. He couldn't wait to see Sally.

We all poked out our heads from the car in anticipation of seeing the dogs. Usually, Sally came dancing out to greet him, but this time, there was nothing.

"Sal Bitch!" he called. "Here, Sal Bitch." Still nothing.

My father returned to the car, pulling it into the garage. We spilled out, calling for Sally. Finally, after several minutes of searching and calling, my father saw that the pantry door in the garage was ajar, when it was usually closed. By now we were all back in the garage crowding behind my father as he peeked into the darkness of the pantry.

"Sally!" he called one more time. She didn't answer, but we could feel her presence. He switched on the light.

Curled up in the back corner under a bottom shelf, barely alive, lay his beloved Sally. There was blood all around her. She had been attacked, either by another dog or maybe a coyote. She weakly lifted her little head, her eyes squinting in the light. We didn't know how long she had been bleeding in that dark and lonely corner.

My father, tears streaming down his face, wrapped his precious dog in a blanket and rushed her to the nearest animal hospital. He returned alone. Sally had lost too much blood and couldn't be saved. My father was grief-stricken. The one thing he loved, knew how to love, was gone.

The whole family wept, except for me. I sat on my bed sorry and horrified that Sally had suffered but unable to share in their sorrow, as if that poor little dog really had anything to do with the troubles between my father and me.

Like most people in those days, we rarely used seat belts. Mom and I were barreling down Carnelian on our way to a hair appointment in our blue Ford station wagon when an elderly man ran the stop sign on Banyan and we crashed into the driver's side of his car. When I got thrown forward on impact, my face went through the windshield and back again through the glass shards, ripping part of my face. Warm blood streamed down the right side of my face. I couldn't see and pushed my finger through what I thought was my eye socket. My mom ran around to my side of the car to look at my eye. I calmly informed her that I had lost my right eye.

"You didn't lose your eye, honey. There's just a lot of blood."

Lying to spare me any more trauma, she insisted she could see my eye behind all the blood. I'm sure in her mind she began salvaging my face, telling herself that glass eyes were greatly improved.

Apparently having heard the crash, a woman appeared like an angel somewhere from the middle of one of the groves. The minute she saw the condition of my face, she disappeared back into the grove to find a phone to call an ambulance.

I began feeling weaker. The ambulance hadn't arrived. The woman reappeared, this time with a car. She drove me to the ER, where our family doctor waited.

I was wheeled into the emergency room with something like cheesecloth across my face, smelling my own blood, feeling claustrophobic and nauseous. It took two hours for my doctor to sew fifty stitches into the right side of my eye. I never complained. I stayed in the hospital for a couple of days. My classmates came to visit me. My mother never came.

Months later, I asked my father what the chances were that anything would ever happen to us again on that street.

"One in a million," he said.

CHAPTER 14:

An Impossible Woman

My mother was a social climber, something that emerged fully when we moved to Bella Vista Road. All of her California friends were wealthier than she was. She was a stay-at-home mom, bored and angry that my dad frequently missed work. She believed his absences prevented him from earning the kind of money someone in his profession should. Without a generous income, she thought, she was denied the social status of her friends and the ability to spend money on the kind of clothes and accessories her friends enjoyed.

One solution was to work. She often helped a friend who was an interior decorator, so when this friend offered her a job, it seemed like a no-brainer.

"Absolutely not," my father said, reacting with pride as he informed his wife that she was not going to humiliate him. Since my mom was no feminist, she acquiesced.

I got the brunt of Mom's frustration and meanness. In the darkness of our family room one morning, the patio sliding glass door's curtain closed, Mom placed her hands on my shoulder and said, "You know I love you but prefer boys. Don't you?"

She never slapped my brothers or banished them to their bedrooms the way she did with me. When she called for

Ron, he replied, "You rang?" She found this hilarious; all of us did. And I had felt her preference for my brothers for a long time. But to have it confirmed was devastating. I stood there paralyzed until she walked away.

Back in my room, I closed the door and started to cry. I appeased myself thinking, *I'm Daddy's favorite.*

A couple days later, we were driving in my mother's car, the Thunderbird. My window was down and I was enjoying the breeze. Out of nowhere, she said, "I asked Cecille, 'Who do you think is prettier, me or Deb?'" Cecille was my mother's childhood friend. Mother looked at me and said, "Cecille said I was."

This time, I didn't feel hurt. I saw her as pathetic to feel she was in competition with her fourteen-year-old daughter. Plus, I thought she was prettier than me, too.

It didn't stop with emotional harm. There was physical violence, too. One evening, I decided to make chocolate pudding. Our mixer stood in a cupboard on a retractable shelf, which could be pulled out and up and snapped into position. Apparently, I had not secured it. The next thing I knew, mixer, bowl, and pudding crashed to the floor, chocolate splattering everywhere.

My mother heard and raced into the kitchen, white with rage. She pounded me with her fist, screaming, "Damn you! Look at this mess. You broke my mixer!" She started to cry and screamed at my father to get me out of her sight.

My father intervened, pulling her off me.

As he tried to console her with "I can buy you another mixer," I ran to my room and shut the door. I sat on my bed sobbing, scared and furious, muttering to myself what a bitch my mother was. I could hear her sobbing and shouting to my father that he better not let me near her.

Finally, my bedroom door opened. My father walked over and sat down beside me on my purple and lavender bedspread and put his arm around me.

"I want to kill her," I sobbed. "I want to take a knife and stab her to death."

"I'll bet you do," he said. "It's okay to think that."

It felt good telling him that. It felt even better that he let me say it with impunity. This was a moment of clarity, because I realized he felt the same way. She was an impossible woman. But it wasn't just my mother who was verbally and physically abusive. They both were. Other times, they spoiled us. They were rarely on the same side in their parenting, which made everything unpredictable and frightening.

Sometimes my mom and I had fun. Twice a year we drove to Bullock's in Pasadena for shopping and lunch in the tea-room on the top floor. Shopping and lunch were what we did best together. I wasn't greedy, and she was generous. She loved to buy me everything. Our last shopping spree in the summer of 1964 was no different. She hauled armloads of jumpers, dresses, and coordinated ensembles into the cramped dressing room.

Of course, I wanted everything, but I didn't press. Instead, I said, "This is so much stuff."

"What do you like best?" she asked. "Pick the three outfits you like best."

My eyes drifted over the outfits piled on the stool and hanging in our stall. *I can't choose*, I thought to myself. I loved the suede button-down jumper with the gold chain belt and light-blue blouse, the seersucker skirt and top, which I later shrank in the dryer. If my three favorites weren't hers, she bought me almost everything. She couldn't stand not to buy everything that looked good on me.

Purchases made, we rode the escalator to the top floor, bags swinging from our arms. The tearoom was a large, light, and airy room with long windows lining Lake Avenue, overstuffed booths lining the opposite walls, tables for four covered in white linen filling the middle, a small stage off in the corner. We waited for a booth. I was wearing the blue corduroy suit my mom had tailor-made for me. The jacket felt a half size too small over the long-sleeved blouse, but it was an ensemble I loved. I liked feeling coordinated. My hair hung down my back, the front half pulled to a ponytail held in place by a blue silk ribbon. I looked very prim and proper as I slid into the booth on the opposite side of my mom.

We ordered Cokes. The waitress delivered them in tall, slim glasses, a maraschino cherry floating on top of the ice cubes clinking against the glass, a straw rising above the glass like a periscope.

The straw was my favorite part. I had a ritual with my mom. First, I lifted my straw from my glass, tore the top of the white paper casing off, stuck an open end in my mouth, pointed it directly at my mother, and blew the casing across the table, hitting her right in the face. Mom found this routine hilarious.

A man in the booth behind us laughed, too, remarking that I looked too charming and refined to blow the casing of a straw into my mother's face. She loved this. She told this story over and over. "I saw him admiring her when we sat down," she began. "When she blew that straw across the table into my face, he couldn't believe it." She laughed, relishing the contradiction.

These were my favorite moments. I wished she were that way all the time. More often she was preoccupied with her own affairs and intolerant of her children.

Meanwhile, my father was not adjusting well to his only daughter becoming a teenager. At breakfast one morning, he groused at my white lipstick. "Wipe that stuff off your face," he demanded. I was frightened, but my mom stuck up for me, saying, "Leave her alone, Cork," which he did.

One day, he brought a beautiful wooden table and chairs home for me. The set was too big for a small child and too little for a teenager. I felt embarrassed and angry that he was treating me like a little girl when I was fourteen. Surreptitiously, my mother made fun of him, telling me, "He doesn't get it, does he, Debbie?"

CHAPTER 15:

Orphans

A few days after my mother's arrest, Joan Lance took us back to our house to collect some belongings. I ran to my bedroom sobbing and fell spread-eagle on my single bed, hands clutching the sides. I screamed "no" over and over again. When Mrs. Lance entered my room, I clutched the sides of my bed even tighter. I knew I would never live in this house again if I let her take me away, and I had no plans to let go. Mrs. Lance tried to comfort me, reaching over me to peel my hands from my bed, but I wouldn't let go. To do so meant leaving everything I'd ever known. Between sobs, I begged, "This is my home. Please don't take me from my home."

Initially, I imagined an acquittal and my mother coming home. I imagined she'd resume raising us. Every day, however, the news headlines made things look worse: "Divorce Action by Dead Dentist's Wife Disclosed," "Defense Expects Drug Claim in Dentist Case," "Dentist Under Drug Influence Jury Will Hear," and finally "Dentist's Wife Denied Plea to Attend Funeral."

As the days and weeks passed after her arrest, it became clear that my mother wasn't coming home any time soon.

Another devastating blow was the interruption of our education. Before my father's death, I'd studied hard and earned good grades. Afterward, I barely attended school. Because I attended my mother's trial, I missed most of tenth grade. My math teacher invited me to her home on weekends to help me stay caught up, but she mostly baked chocolate cookies for me and tried to soothe my sorrows.

After my mother's conviction and incarceration, I yearned to leave Los Angeles, leave the publicity, the eyes in my church condemning my mother, the comments that humiliated, the anger I felt. The summer after my sophomore year, I managed to get out of Los Angeles for a Seventh-day Adventist boarding school in Northern California in Healdsburg, a small town in the Napa Valley.

My grades began to drop right away my junior year. The only class I liked was typing. The trial and its aftermath interrupted my education to such a degree that I would never fully engage in any of my classes again.

In December 1964, two months after her arrest, the jury selection for my mother's trial began. While her attorneys met with her every day, my brothers and I had not been allowed to see her. At that time, officials did not designate a place where parents who were in jail and children could meet and hold each other, a place where parents could remind their kids how much they loved and missed them, a place where they could explain the situation as best they could and allay their loved ones' fears as much as possible, then hug and kiss and cry together. Children simply weren't allowed in the jail, and we were desperate without her.

Options emerged for where the Miller children should live. Sandy stepped forward, but immediately, criticism of her materialized. She was too young. She was in medical school and needed to concentrate on that. She wasn't qualified. She wasn't family. Sandy wanted to move back into our house and keep us. Sandy was like a sister and was our first choice. We loved her and knew she loved us. Our lives would have been less disrupted if Sandy had been allowed to be our guardian. After all, Sandy was smart and a medical student. She understood our family and our habits.

But it was not to be.

The Lances offered to keep us, but then, unfortunately, my father's sister, Genevera Thompson, stepped forward to take the boys. She and her family lived in Washington State. My brothers didn't know these people. Worst of all, they were strict Seventh-day Adventists and saw our family as the black sheep, gone wicked once we'd moved to California. But they were family, and no one could tell them no.

Before my brothers left to live with my aunt and uncle, we finally were allowed to see our mom. An arrangement was made for us to visit her in the sheriff's office at the San Bernardino courthouse. We were led in through thick oak doors to a large room with green shag carpet and a huge oak desk. Everything was hushed. Guy and Ronnie wore little checkered shirts and chinos. All Brylcreemed up, each of their little crew cuts looked like a newly planted lawn.

Frightened and confused but stoic, the boys stood in this big room barely looking at each other, arms hanging at their sides, faces scrubbed and ready to say goodbye to their mom. The oak door opened. Our mother entered the room, hands cuffed in front of her, wearing a drab wrap-around dress issued from the jail. But she wore makeup, her hair styled in a French twist.

She'd thought of details to prepare for this meeting. The care she took with her appearance probably lifted her spirits and was meant to lift ours and put us at ease, too. She didn't want her children to see her like this, something the penal system didn't give a damn about. We were devastated. The last thing she wanted was to send us away or make things any worse for us than it was already. For us to see her fixed up, even if it wasn't the complete look we were used to, banished some of our fear. She was about to send her children off to live with relatives and friends they hardly knew. She did not know what the future for her or her children looked like, or when or if she would ever be our mother again. The possibility of us crying and clinging to her was unthinkable. Everything had to appear safe and temporary.

Two female officers escorted her into the room, guided her to a chair, and helped her sit down. One of them removed the handcuffs.

We were given maybe a half hour to spend with her. The guards left, closing the door behind them, leaving us alone with Mom, whom we hadn't seen or talked to in two months. I was a devout Christian, which served me well as it gave me hope and strength. I wrote my mother letters telling her I was praying and she should pray, too, and that God was on our side.

At the beginning of our visit, nobody made a move or a sound. I stared at my mother's long, graceful fingers and hands, her nails still long, squared at the tip, polished a cheap pearl pink. Somehow, she'd managed a manicure. The color must have been the one available for female convicts, because she painted her nails the same through her trial and the years she spent in prison. Her face was thin and pale, her eyes sunken and dead. She must have felt humiliated. I felt humiliated for her and wanted to rush into her arms, but I sat paralyzed.

Things began awkwardly, with us asking each other, "How are you doing?"—a question nobody answered honestly.

"It's hard to eat," my mother began. She was a vegetarian. The mess they cooked in jail mostly contained chicken or beef.

She had tried asking for hard-boiled eggs or cottage cheese. Sometimes she was accommodated; mostly she wasn't.

That was about as negative as she got. Mom assured us she would be coming home, that we'd all be home together soon. We believed her.

She tried to explain why Guy and Ronnie were being sent away. "I've always loved Genevera," she began. "Your auntie Genevera is very nice to take you. They have a big house, a big yard. You'll like it. You'll get to play in the snow."

None of this was working, of course. My brothers just sat there nodding.

"When will we be able to come home?" Guy asked.

"As soon as this is over," Mom replied.

"This" came to mean a lot of things, the unspoken things. That day, "this" meant legal proceedings. Later, it meant the allegation of murder, and later still, a trial. Those abstractions didn't mean anything to us yet. Each "this" was a component unto itself. "This" went on and on. It was easier not to call anything by its name, which made it too real, too unbearable. This was momentary, doable. Anybody could do this for a while.

My mother turned to me and said, "You're old enough to make your own decision about where you want to live."

We did our part. Whatever doubts we had, we did not express. She was setting the example of how we were to conduct ourselves, and without her having to say anything, we knew what to do. The conversation that day was polite. She assured my brothers they were going on a big adventure and that when they got home, she would be waiting for them. By the time we left, we actually thought everything she said was true—that our life's path was taking nothing more than a small detour. We would all be together again soon. We accepted this was reason enough not to complain.

Our visit ended as stoically as it had begun. We all hugged, but not tightly. We didn't cry, not then. We might all fall apart. A quick hug was meant to reinforce the ephemeral position we were in. Little did we know our family, our life together, was essentially over.

My aunt and uncle didn't love my brothers, and I missed them terribly. My aunt and uncle believed we were spoiled. They saw my parents, particularly my mother, as far worldlier than the rest of our family. They did not approve of my mother's makeup, wedding band, or fashionable clothes. We lived in California, a heathen state, with too much Hollywood influence. We actually lived in what Hollywood considered the sticks of California, but our relatives didn't know this and didn't want to.

Several of my mom's friends offered to let me stay with them. After all, this was only temporary, wasn't it? I was lucky. I was allowed to find my new home, and I knew just where I wanted to go.

Yolande and Eddie Ford, friends of my mom, were my first choice. Yolande had once hired me to help her with a dinner party. I'd joyfully served her guests dinner and scoured her kitchen. I had known my place and didn't try to insert myself into her party, even though I had grown up with all of the guests, and I could scrub down a kitchen like nobody's business. I made a good impression.

Yolande was my idol, and I jumped at the chance to live with them when they offered.

My mother's arrest and indictment remained headline news. I intended to steel myself against the effects. The only power I'd been given was to choose where I wanted to live. I didn't want another family. I didn't want rules or a routine. I didn't want people trying to make my life seem normal.

I wasn't going to pretend that it was. So my instinct to move to the Fords' house proved right for me.

Yolande Ford was French, and before marrying Eddie, she'd enjoyed a glamorous life. She'd been a model and dated famous people, like one of the Hilton brothers and the actor Hugh O'Brian. It was exciting, at least to me, to know someone who had dated famous people. I loved her stories. She told me that by day, she had worn white and assisted a doctor. By night, she had dined with her famous boyfriends at the landmark Perino's on Wilshire or the Brown Derby.

I loved that her story always ended with how empty she felt, how she felt she was going nowhere until friends introduced her to a young doctor named Eddie. Dr. Eddie Ford attended our church, and the day he arrived with his new bride on his arm, we were all agog. Not only was she more beautiful than anyone we had ever seen, but she was gracious and warm. She became our local star. My mother took her directly under her wing. Yolande had everything my mother wanted, but my mother was also a friendly person, and she introduced her to all of her friends.

The Fords lived in a modern glass house on stilts on the side of a hill in the flashy part of Cucamonga known as Red Hill. The neighborhood's streets wound around the hill to the Red Hill Golf Course and Country Club, the Bel Air of Cucamonga. Their house was mostly living room, all glass, providing an expansive view of groves and empty fields in the daytime and at night the sparkle of a city still in its infancy. Having lost my own house, I couldn't think of a better place to live.

No one in the Ford house sat down for a meal. No one cooked. I lived on Rice Krispies squares, which was fine with me. Sometimes Mrs. Ford deep-fried a batch of homemade french fries. No one told me when to go to bed or to do my homework. Practically nothing was expected of me. I wanted to be Yolande Ford. I wanted Mrs. Ford's closets full of clothes, her vanity of expensive creams and perfumes. I wanted to dab my cheeks and forehead in the middle of the day with a tiny wax hanky to remove shine from oils on my face. I watched Mrs. Ford carefully, how she stood up straight, regularly rotating her shoulders gently into place, and making a funny little sound clearing her nose. I loved to watch her hands, manicured but strong and graceful. She was glamorous, down to her lime-green Cadillac convertible.

The months at the Fords' house, their generosity and love for me, softened a bitter heart. Their easiness with me, accompanying me to my mother's trial, trusting and believing that I was an okay kid, was an early step toward survival.

Despite the loose rules, I was a responsible teenager. My faith in God, my prudishness and inherent good sense, kept me out of trouble. However, I was scared all the time.

One sign of my anxiety was cleaning my dirty fingernails with my teeth. I developed worms. Humiliated and frightened, I didn't know what to do. I kept my problem a secret until it became unbearable for me. I was raw from itching, and it got to the point where I actually saw them wiggling in my poop. I was convinced I had some terrible disease. Finally, one night, I went sobbing to Mrs. Ford, sure that I was dying or starving because the worms were eating away at me. She allayed my fears, assuring me that my picking and eating at myself all the time had caused the worms and that the condition was easily cured. I begged her not to tell Dr. Ford. She promised discretion and kept her promise, procuring the medicine for me without his ever saying one word to me.

The worst part of this time was how desperate I was to see my brothers. No one even set up phone calls between us. It didn't occur to us to write or send letters.

CHAPTER 16:

Mistrial

My mother's case was moving through the system as news of it reached a wide audience through stories in the *Los Angeles Times* and *Herald Examiner*. Harold Lance wanted to hire as my mother's lawyer John King, a well-known and respected criminal attorney in San Bernardino County and owner of King Ranch above Bella Vista Road, a gruff, no-nonsense attorney who won cases. At the time, Harold was one of the attorneys in a civil trial. John King was the attorney for the other side. John King fell to the ground during the trial and died of a heart attack.

Instead, Edward Foley was hired to defend her because of his gentle nature. Foley was Irish, a charming and handsome fair-skinned man with beautiful silver-white hair and roseate cheeks lined with tiny veins. While his kindness and tenderness bucked up my mom, it wasn't the kind of temperament to win an acquittal. He was so convinced of her innocence, he couldn't see that a jury might convict her. My mother was not a sympathetic defendant. She appeared arrogant. Even though she was in jail, she found a way to wear nice clothes, her hair always well-coiffed. She did not cry. King believed that women defendants ought to cry, and his approach might have softened the hearts of the jury. Would that have resulted in an acquittal? Of course, we'll never know.

Sandy and I thought Foley didn't object enough. Each day after the trial, Sandy, following every detail, gave him written notes listing what he should have done. He ignored her advice. He didn't discourage my mom's stoicism or caution her about her appearance. Her manner was too cold, her hair too well-coiffed, her clothes too stylish, her nails too manicured. We should have fired him.

The first major development in the case came in December 1964 when Judge Carl B. Hilliard declared a mistrial. His decision hinged on a leak to the press about the death of Elaine Hayton, the wife of my mother's lover. Sheriff Frank Bland was the leaker. He shared that my mother had been the last person to see her alive, creating an opportunity for my mother's attorney to argue that the leak made it impossible for her to get a fair trial.

I was living at the Fords' and spending time with my new friend, Julie Mandala, who lived across the street. I did not know about the mistrial, what that meant, or why it was needed. Whoever told me about it explained the situation as though it didn't mean anything.

Years later, I read the transcripts, in which Mr. Foley articulated the rationale for the mistrial:

> ***The Court:*** *Mr. Foley, this session of the court was called at your request.*
>
> ***Mr. Foley:*** *Yes, Your Honor. I was quite shocked last evening shortly before five o'clock to receive a telephone call from Jack Hartsfield [a San Bernardino]*

> *Sun-Telegram Staff Writer . . . asking me if I had any comment on The [headline] "Was Wife of San Bernardino Attorney Murdered" . . . [that] appeared [in the] San Bernardino Sun, [along with] . . . A subline [that] states: "Mrs. Hayton's Death Linked to Miller Case." To my knowledge, she has never been quizzed in the probe of Elaine Hayton's death at all. The introduction of the affair coupled now with all the implications in the death of Elaine Hayton, the suspicion that is on my client for her murder absolutely prevents me from getting a fair trial. I am going to ask the court to declare a mistrial.*

The judge agreed.

The connection between my family and the Haytons went back to when we first moved to California and my mother's request that the teacher introduce me to the most popular girl in first grade. My friendship with Terry Hayton brought our families together. Both families attended the small Adventist church in Ontario. Arthwell was a prominent local attorney, Elaine a former nurse. Elaine and my mom were stay-at-home moms, and both were active in our church and in our community. The Hayton and Miller families often took trips to the beach together and cruises on Arthwell's boat, my mother slyly taking on the role of hostess, trotting around, head held high. I felt uncomfortable during these gatherings. I wondered if Elaine suspected my mother's betrayals, if Terry noticed the obnoxious behavior between my mother and her father.

Because of my mother's friendship with Elaine, she learned early on that Arthwell was a philanderer. At the same time that she was having an affair with Elaine's husband, my mother was becoming Elaine's confidante. On one occasion, Elaine found a bracelet on the floor of their car. Weeping, she called my mother, who rushed to Elaine's rescue. If my mom and Elaine weren't best friends before the mysterious bracelet was discovered, they became the closest of confidantes after that.

This deceitful behavior was driven by my mom's belief that Arthwell needed to leave Elaine and marry her. Mom felt she was better prepared to be the wife of a prominent lawyer. But Arthwell informed Mom that he loved Elaine and would never leave her.

On that night in April 1964 when our phone rang and Elaine tearfully asked my mother to come talk to her, Arthwell was away. He had taken his boat to Catalina to celebrate their oldest son's birthday. The two other Hayton boys, Bruce and Geoff, were asleep, and Terry was at choir practice, so there were no witnesses to what happened that night between the two women.

It was my parents who went to pick up Terry from choir practice that night. They must have gone to get her because Elaine was upset, but I never really knew. What I do know is that early the next morning, our phone rang. It was Terry. She had found her mother and couldn't wake her up. She told me later that she knew immediately her mother was dead. My mother told me that Elaine had committed suicide. In fact, she died of an overdose, but it was inconclusive as to whether she overdosed intentionally or by accident.

Terry had her own story to tell later. According to her, there was a chill inside of that car when my parents picked her up. My mom, always abundantly loving to Terry, was cold; no one spoke, the usual chattering and laughing languished somewhere in the past. When they arrived back at the Haytons' house, my mother followed her in and stood by the door to Elaine's bedroom. Unable to find any toothpaste in the kids' bathroom, Terry wandered to her parents' room for toothpaste, but my mother stopped her at the door, telling Terry her mother was asleep and shouldn't be disturbed. Terry explained she regularly used her parents' toothpaste when the kids' supply ran out. My mother stiffened. She wasn't Terry's dear Auntie Lucille. She stood her ground, refusing to let Terry into the bedroom or bathroom.

Angry and disconcerted, Terry went to bed while my mother continued standing in the hall. Terry finally heard the front door close as she drifted off to sleep.

I attended Elaine's funeral with my mother and father. Arthwell had ended their affair months before, but my mother strolled to the Hayton pew and sat with Arthwell and his children. I could feel the tension all around me, a quiet hush. I sat with my father and my brothers in the back. I was humiliated for my father and enraged at my mother.

After Elaine's death, Arthwell lost interest in my mother. She couldn't believe it and wouldn't accept it. She called him at his office until he told his secretary not to put her calls through to him. One day, she showed up at Arthwell's house and packed up the clothes of Geoff Hayton, the youngest boy. She told the governess that Arthwell had given her permission to pick him up. No one questioned her. Geoff cheerfully jumped into Auntie Lucille's car and went missing for more than a week.

In the transcripts, Arthwell testified he'd never given my mother permission to pick up his son and that he had no idea when she intended to bring Geoff home, although he knew they were at a cabin in Big Bear. When asked why he didn't demand his son's return, he said he didn't know how to get to the cabin and didn't know the phone number. He didn't call the police, either, so clearly he wasn't too worried about Geoff's safety.

After this strange event, my mother continued picking up the Hayton kids while threatening to reveal the affair. Arthwell kept trying to dump her, but they continued to meet into July. Then, finally, it stopped.

Mom's betrayal of Elaine and my father caused great suffering. Still, she continued to insist that she was the one Arthwell loved. When it came to him she was, even to her teenage daughter, a silly fool.

I saw Terry in the fall of 1964, shortly before my father's death. She was leaving to attend a Seventh-day Adventist boarding school in Healdsburg, California, and I wouldn't see her again for many years. Before she left, Terry asked to stop and see me and to give me a hug and a kiss. I didn't understand then that I wouldn't see her anymore for years to come, or that the reason was because Arthwell Hayton believed my mother had murdered his wife. I didn't know that Terry also believed my mother had killed her mother, but she loved me enough to say goodbye.

CHAPTER 17:

The Kindness of Strangers

During the Christmas holidays in 1964, before the new trial started, I visited my brothers for the first time. I was excited to see them.

My aunt Genevera was married to Tom Thompson, a dentist. Uncle Tom was tall, with thinning hair but sporting a healthy mustache, a handsome man whose brown eyes sparkled and perfect white teeth gleamed when he smiled.

My mother claimed Genevera had been beautiful when she was young, but to me she looked ghostly and stern. She had suffered with rheumatic fever in early childhood, was tall and pale, her eyes dull, deep lines running from her nose to her chin. Her hair, colorless and a bit fuzzy, lay limp and closely cropped to her head. My father was her baby brother and her favorite. It was an open secret that my uncle Tom did not treat her well and that she had a heart condition as a result of the rheumatic fever. She was often bedridden.

When we were growing up, my father had taken us to Walla Walla a few times. My aunt and uncle lived outside town on quiet roads, the pavement hot and simmering. We'd cut through giant fields of green or yellow that flowed until swallowed by the horizon. My aunt and uncle's massive lawn undulated in small mounds away from the house, a single-story series of rectangles sprawling in every direction. The house was no different now, except snow covered the landscape like a down quilt. Their house smelled like our house on a Friday night, dried beans locked in a pressure cooker on the stove, freshly baked cherry pies on the counter. A sense of security and familiarity settled around me. It felt like home.

But now, my little brothers painted a very different picture. They came to the room I was sleeping in that first night in their pajamas and crew cuts to sit on my bed and weep. They begged me to find a way to get them out of that house. They told me that for minor infractions, my aunt would send them out to the willow tree to choose a branch, which then was used to whip them, leaving welts. They said my uncle had decided that the way to make a man out of a nine-year-old was to drill his teeth without Novocain. My brothers had become nervous wrecks and constantly frightened.

This scene played out each night I was there, desperate to pour their hearts out to someone who loved them and would listen to them.

We were unaware that many people were working fast and furiously behind the scenes to take care of us and not let the courts intervene. My mother was about to go to trial. The Miller children's circumstances were considered temporary, so the best temporary plan for our well-being was set in place. Harold and Joan Lance did everything they could to follow my mother's wishes. Many people came forward offering to take care of us until our mother's trial was over. No one doubted that she would be acquitted. There didn't seem to be a plan for if she didn't come home, so certain everyone was that things would end well.

On my first night with the Fords, Yolande Ford and I arrived home from the courthouse to find Julie Mandala, a beautiful young Italian girl my age who lived across the street and babysat the Fords' two children, Christian and Michael, sitting on the couch. She wore a faux leopard swing coat, her Sophia Loren face accentuated with orange lip gloss. She looked gorgeous, and my first reaction was to hate her. Her beauty was bad enough, but that Mrs. Ford was thrilled to see her, the obvious fondness they shared for each other, made her a threat.

Many years later, I found out Julie was jealous of me, believing I was taking Yolande away from her. If she had told me that at the time, I wouldn't have been able to fathom it. I was astounded that Julie addressed Mrs. Ford as Yolande. I had grown up calling adults Mr. and Mrs. It seemed cheap of this girl to refer to Mrs. Ford by her first name. But by the next morning, Mrs. Ford had become Yolande to me, too.

Julie was Catholic. Adventists held a special abhorrence for Catholics, fearing a modern-day Inquisition that would target them. So I was instinctively afraid of Catholics. Fortunately, all of my fears and prejudices eventually changed. Julie became my best friend and her family my adopted family. I was learning about families who were different from mine—more loving and affectionate, less rigid. I was seeing what it was like to have fun in a family and not be afraid all the time.

Julie was the youngest of four: Her oldest brother, Chuck, was married. Frank lived at home and helped run the family business. Rosalie, another beauty who also lived at home and shared a bedroom with Julie, attended Chaffey Junior College. They were not a perfect family. The Mandala children were first-generation Americans. The hierarchy in their Italian family gave Julie and Rosie's brothers power over them, setting their curfew, deciding whom Julie and Rosie could date. While I found this unbelievable, the sisters took it in stride because it wasn't a rigid arrangement. They were a little community, something I hadn't experienced. In spite of the macho male control in their family, Julie felt loved.

The beauty in the family came from Julie's mom, Nina. I never understood how Mr. Mandala convinced her to marry him. Julie's dad was an alcoholic. He had a bulbous nose with tiny red veins crawling all over it. His front teeth needed braces because they folded on top of each other. His Italian accent was so thick that I couldn't understand him, which always made the family laugh and his eyes twinkle. At first, he seemed kind of fierce, but I came to love him. While I officially lived at the Ford house, I ate dinners with Julie and her family most nights and eventually ended up sleeping primarily at their house, too.

They seemed so worldly compared to my sheltered life. Everyone loved to laugh. There always seemed to be a fight at the dinner table from which I recoiled, sending them all into fits of laughter.

"This is how Italians talk," Rosie explained between the laughter and the shouting. "We're loud! We shout!"

They were an excitable and volatile bunch. Julie's mom spent most of her days cooking. I learned that spaghetti was a side dish, not an entrée. I slurped down bowls of homemade minestrone soup, another side dish, and eagerly awaited dinner, when I'd find Julie's mom in the kitchen pounding veal, dipping it in eggs and then breadcrumbs for veal parmesan. Everyday dishes made by Julie's mom were served on Franciscan ware, creamy porcelain with painted pink flowers and green leaves lining the outside. I fell in love with these dishes. They became a symbol to me of Julie's family, their love and all that good cooking. Many years later, Julie's mom gave me those dishes.

In spite of the Mandalas' love and acceptance, I found myself uncomfortable around their extended family and friends. Julie grew up working the snack bar on the shore of Lake Arrowhead. Her family purchased a house near the lake and spent their summers working and water-skiing. One day, Rosie's rich ex-boyfriend invited us all to his house with its own dock to water-ski. I felt like an outsider. I felt like a third arm, the tagalong, the poor orphan. I was afraid to speak, laugh, or enjoy myself too much. I was afraid to ask to use the bathroom in a stranger's house. I clung to Julie. I didn't want her out of my sight. I wouldn't try anything new. They all water-skied without a care in the world. After being hounded one afternoon, I gave it a try, but I failed and felt foolish. The only thing fun to me was racing around in Julie's brother Frankie's red speedboat. When he sensed my discomfort, Frankie loaded me into his boat and tore around that lake. He couldn't go fast enough for me. I loved the wind blowing my hair straight back. I loved whizzing by all the mansions surrounding the lake, the glory of the woods, the tall pines.

I attended my first mass, a midnight mass, on Christmas Eve 1966, with Julie, Rosalie, and their mom and dad. The night was cold, stars shining bright. A soft yellow light emanated from inside their church. We were bundled up in our winter best. Rosie wore a black hat, like a Russian Cossack. All three Mandala women wore fur coats. Mr. Mandala wore a fedora and winter coat. We found a pew near the front.

Someone was playing Christmas music on the organ as the church filled up. The altar was decorated with red poinsettias. Soon the priest rose from his chair and approached the altar table. While the entire ceremony was alien to me, I loved it, all of it, standing, kneeling, and standing again, the congregation answering the priest, speaking together, the singing and organ music. I so wanted to celebrate the Eucharist along with everyone else.

That winter, the Mandalas took over the snack bar in Snow Valley. Since I was considered part of their family, I spent weekends with them, working as the cashier. I mostly never counted the change correctly, choosing instead to let the customers count their own change. I also hated skiing. Like so much else in the world, it scared me. I never had the proper clothes or ski equipment like Julie and Rosalie. I was bundled up in whatever extra clothing could be found. My boots, poles, and skis were rented. Feeling pieced together made me think I couldn't ski. Even when the Mandalas paid for ski lessons for me, I couldn't get the hang of it and never got beyond snowplowing all the way down the bunny hill.

CHAPTER 18:

The Trial

Mom's trial continued to be delayed. She had been arrested the morning of October 8, 1964, and her first trial didn't begin until December 2, 1964. Then came the mistrial, and the new one wouldn't begin until January 11, 1965.

During most of these months, my mom wasn't feeling well. She felt nauseated and lost her appetite. On December 18, 1964, Dr. Joseph Langer arrived at the jail to examine her. The next day, we learned that Mom was pregnant.

All of us latched on to the news of Mom's pregnancy as the good omen I had been praying for every day. I created a fantasy that no jury would convict her. We would all be together again and love this baby, a gift from God, a new family.

I watched her tummy grow during the trial. She weighed less than one hundred pounds, and I was frantic about her stress and trauma and the jail's unwillingness to fully accommodate her pregnancy. She later told me they never gave her enough milk, so she saved cartons that sometimes soured. In an interview recorded many years later, her voice trembled as she recounted bad food and cockroaches in her cell. Her lawyers would sneak in tomatoes for her, but it wasn't enough. I worried constantly. She looked so tiny and vulnerable.

This was not her former lover's baby. That relationship had ended long before my father's death. She and my father were trying to make the marriage work. They were actively working to make a baby as part of the better life they intended to create. I learned this in court.

At fourteen, I never doubted her innocence. I never imagined she was wicked. She was so little, that little bump protruding, her face drawn, her eyes sad. She looked for me every time she walked into the courtroom. My heart soared that she loved me.

On the first day of my mother's trial, I conjured a plan. It didn't take long for me to execute it. Leaning against the wall next to the courtroom in the San Bernardino County courthouse, I came dressed in a navy-blue skirt and kelly-green sweater. I had not seen our mother since our short visit in the sheriff's office just before my brothers left for Walla Walla. My adrenaline was pumping because my plan was to rush to my mother as deputies led her from her jail cell to the courtroom, handcuffed and pregnant.

I was going to embrace her no matter what. The whole world was waiting there with me—attorneys, the press, the public—but it was as if I were the only one left in the world, knowing my mother would pass by at any second. Attendance at my mother's trial was already a problem, with spectators pushing and shoving each other, one day breaking the glass of the courtroom doors in the madness to attend the trial.

I was oblivious to the chaos on this day, however. I remained motionless, against the wall, like a fan waiting for the arrival of her rock star. Finally, I saw her approaching, a female deputy holding her elbow on one side, a male deputy holding her elbow on the other side, her hands clasped in front of her, locked in handcuffs. She looked beautiful, wearing a little makeup, her hair stylishly combed in a flip.

I caught my mother's eye, the corner of my mouth curling into a half smile.

Unbelievably, no one was blocking me. The moment she reached the wall across from where I stood, she paused for a split second.

I was desperate to touch my mom. Crashing through all of the camera lights flashing, the media shouting questions at me when they realized what was happening, the officers trying to keep Mom out of my reach, I dashed over to her, cupped my hands around her tiny face, and kissed her on the lips. Her hands reached out to embrace me, but she'd forgotten she was handcuffed; she formed a two-handed fist and rested it against my chest. In a picture taken by the *Los Angeles Times*, a female deputy smiles, almost as if posing for the camera, while a male deputy, shocked and caught off-guard, reaches to separate us. Mom and I both burst into tears. I was so proud to have overcome the obstacles trying to keep me away from her.

Prosecutor Don Turner asked for the death penalty at the new trial, as he had the first time, but he'd failed to mention that she was pregnant. What we, the family, did not know was that this harsh stance was a ploy to help him assure a jury likely to issue a guilty verdict. By asking for the death penalty, he was able to eliminate any potential juror who had an objection to it. This became a major point of contention on appeal. But during the whole trial, all I knew was that he wanted to kill my mother.

I believed throughout the trial that if my mother were convicted, she would be executed. This terror I experienced every day in court, and the suffering Turner caused my brothers and me during those many months, made him forever a wicked man.

The trial would be mostly about my feelings, and the atmosphere of tension and fear. The actual ins and outs of it were mostly boring and theoretical. Attending court as much as possible was important to me because I wanted to support my mother and it was the only way I could see her. Mom dreaded what my coming to court and seeing her in handcuffs would do to me, but I needed to witness everything. However, I never kept a journal or record of any kind. For years, I had a small photo album of the pictures I'd collected from the newspaper during the trial in which I had written things like "My poor, poor mother" or "The unfair and unjust trial of my mother."

Years later, as an adult, I pulled them out of the bottom of a closet and looked through them. Reading my comments, I felt embarrassed that they lacked the beauty of a poet and the insight of a psychiatrist. Much to my regret, I threw them away so that no one would ever find them, leaving me with little substantive evidence of my lived experience of those days in the courtroom.

Much of the testimony during the trial was from experts. One issue was the burning car. Defense experts testified that the Volkswagen was not set on fire, rather that the fire had been caused by mechanical failure within the car. Experts for the prosecution asserted that they'd found nothing in the car that would have set it ablaze by accident. I stopped attending the trial on the days of expert testimony.

Other parts of the proceedings were more memorable. It came out that an undercover agent had been planted in my mother's cell. The woman had posed as having been arrested for drugs and prostitution. Peggy Fisk, an undercover cop who worked in narcotics and was employed by the sheriff's office, had tried to convince my mother not to trust her attorneys and to instead throw herself on the mercy of the sheriff. She also told my mother that she "had mistrusted her own attorney and indicated that perhaps [my mother] shouldn't [trust] hers." The sheriff referred to by the informant was the one whose leak to the press had caused a mistrial. On the basis of a number of legitimate legal objections, my mother's attorney could have stopped Peggy Fisk from testifying, but he failed to do so.

Some relief came when my mother's friends defended her on the witness stand. Other odd things appealed to me: I loved looking as nice as possible, showing off my fall wardrobe from Bullock's Pasadena. I liked looking at pictures of myself in the newspapers but pretended I was disgusted with press photographers. I also liked visiting the snack shop for candy bars because everyone knew my name and was friendly. I was a fourteen-year-old in one of the most surreal situations imaginable—my dad was dead, my mom on trial for his murder, and my brothers cast away to uncaring family members. I was trying to be a grown-up, but I was still just a kid.

A dramatic time in the trial was prosecutor Don Turner's cross-examination of Sandy. He kept trying to impeach her. Defense attorney Foley kept objecting. The judge kept sustaining Foley's objections. Turner wanted to argue that my father never wanted the house on Bella Vista. Sandy and both of the Lances countered that my father loved the lot we had bought, tucked up against Mount Baldy, many miles away from everything. Sandy testified that he "liked to take his binoculars and look at the view and the mountains. He liked to walk around. It was out in the country," where he wanted his kids to have horses and a swimming pool.

I loved hearing Sandy defend my mother, but the prosecutor's battle with her was hard to endure. He kept referring to her testimony before the grand jury, comparing it to her testimony on the witness stand. The sharpness of the interaction was unnerving, his persistence at the number of pills she witnessed my father taking and his grilling of her on every detail, including the morning my mother was arrested, trying to poke holes in her testimony about that morning.

Around the middle of February 1965, during the defense's argument, I also took the stand. I fought for composure. Oddly, the thing that most bothered me about attorney Foley was how he referred to my mother as "your mommy." I was fourteen. I addressed her as either Mother or Mom. He was turning me into a baby when I was a teenager. I was furious. At the same time, I recognized he was trying to appeal to the jury's sympathies.

When Don Turner cross-examined me, my heart raced. I hated him so much. As with Sandy, he pointed out the differences between what I had said to the grand jury and what I was saying on the witness stand. I became so exasperated, I finally replied, "I keep forgetting more and more."

Decades later, reading the transcripts, I became even more furious at Ed Foley. Don Turner was a snake in the grass who knowingly made things up, such as claiming that the barbiturate found in Elaine Hayton's body was the same found in my father's body, which, according to the transcripts, was not true. Even when the judge called both attorneys into chambers and warned Turner, he continued inserting misleading information, knowing that Foley would object, but he didn't care because once the jury heard it, it was in their heads, even when the judge told them they must disregard it. Ed Foley was a lightweight compared to Don Turner. I believe he lost my mother's trial more than Turner won it.

The jury deliberated for two days, March 3 and 4, and reached their decision on March 5. I came to court every day and waited. Sandy sat with me and the attorneys. I was more and more frightened as each day passed.

Foley tried to comfort us, to assure us that the longer the jury deliberated, the better for the defense. I wanted to believe him. My plans and dreams depended on my mother's acquittal. Guy, Ron, Mom, and I finally together again. My mom was six months pregnant by the end of the trial. Before the verdict, we were so excited about our new baby, who was due to arrive in June, the gift the new beginning for all of us. The baby's birth would symbolize the washing away of the trauma of being curled up in my mom's stomach as she languished in jail or sat at the defense table charged with murdering her husband. I couldn't face the alternative. But I felt anxiety, fear, and foreboding.

I could get through the trial. Beyond that, my mind refused to go.

On day three, court was called—the jury had reached a verdict. I wore a bright blue corduroy jumper and white blouse. We took our seats. The courtroom was full of spectators. The jury filed in, faces of stone. Certainly, the jury, or at least one member of the jury, would give me a hint, a slight smile or a half nod, some signal to assure me that everything was going to be okay, that it was over now. That's not what happened, and that's when I knew, though I couldn't comprehend what was about to happen.

Once the jury was seated, the judge asked who the foreman was and if the jury had reached a verdict. The foreman replied, "Yes, Your Honor."

The bailiff took the verdict from the foreman and handed it to the clerk, who read, "We, the jury in the above entitled action, find the defendant, Lucille Marie Miller, guilty of the crime of murder in the first degree, as charged in the indictment. Dated: March 5, 1965. K. J. Lauterborn, Foreman."

My mother gasped and cried out, "Oh. My God, no!"

I went into shock, the courtroom swirling as it all became an echo. "Oh, no!" I shrieked from the spectator section. "Oh, no. Oh, no, I'll never see my mother again!" I was sobbing, believing that she would be executed.

Harold Lance rushed for me and carried me out of the courtroom, holding me underneath his arm. Weeping, I tucked myself into him. I could barely walk. Cameras flashed all around me.

And then, I don't remember.

CHAPTER 19:

Kimi Kai

Once my mother was convicted, my brothers and I became wards of the court. While I didn't understand what it all meant, I was terrified of being separated from my brothers. They had the same fear. Living anywhere except our own home was unfathomable.

We were lucky that the Lances stepped in and offered to become our legal guardians. I had heard the words "foster home" being bandied about, and I had no idea what that meant. I should have been more grateful for the Lances' sacrifice, but I was too shell-shocked to appreciate much of anything people were doing for us.

The Lances added a room onto their family room for me. I was thrilled. I left my own beautiful bedroom set behind and moved my parents' bedroom set and their bed into my new room and painted it yellow.

I returned to school. I liked biology, but I didn't put enough work into it and received a C on my first report card. Although my parents didn't care about grades, the Lances supported my desire to earn high grades. By the end of the school year, I was getting an A in biology.

The Lances had a lovely backyard, which at one point included a duck. One of my favorite biology class assignments was catching insects to mount them and list their scientific information. I found all my insects in their backyard. I screeched, shivered, and jumped every time I had to catch one. The bright green katydid was the most beautiful. Holding a jar, I quietly followed it around until I was able to trap it, creeping myself out the entire time.

My mother entered prison in March 1965, and on June 6, my little sister was born at St. Joseph's Hospital in San Bernardino. My mother didn't want her baby to carry the stigma of being born in prison, so her attorneys petitioned Governor Edmund Brown to allow her to give birth in a hospital. He granted the petition, and my mother became the first incarcerated woman in California to give birth to her child outside of prison.

St. Joseph's offered its facilities after the Seventh-day Adventist, our religion, rejected my mother's request to have the baby in their hospital in Loma Linda. The Adventist church was too busy trying to find a way to excommunicate my mother and didn't want anything to do with us. But the Catholics at St. Joseph's, the dear nuns running that hospital, opened their doors and their arms to my mother.

My brothers and I were not allowed to be present at Kimi's birth. My mother later told me guards were posted everywhere, but she recalled how lovingly those nuns treated her, brushing the security aside, demanding a little respect for mother and child. Mom only stayed in St. Joseph's a few days, but she would always remember that time as wonderful, a respite from the ordeal of the previous many months.

Yet she understood that precious baby girl, whom she declared "the most beautiful baby" of all her children, with her curly black hair, huge brown eyes, and long eyelashes, would not be leaving with her. Mom wanted to name her Tonya but allowed me to overrule her, and our baby became Kimi Kai Miller.

CHAPTER 20:

Survival

In a Frank O'Connor short story, "My Oedipus Conflict," the narrator recalls World War I as "the most peaceful time of my life." His father was away fighting, and he had his mother to himself. I, too, experienced peace during my mom's seven-year incarceration. I was content to know where she was, to know she would be happy to see me, and to know that during our visits, I shared her with no one.

In the days immediately following my mother's conviction, we weren't allowed to visit. My best friend Stephanie and her family had just moved to Gilroy, California, famous for its garlic and artichoke crops. The Lances likely thought it would be good for me to visit Stephanie while we were waiting for my mom to be processed, to leave town for a few days and soak in some love and friendship after the shock of Mom's guilty verdict. I thought so, too.

The Lances drove me to Gilroy, a long way from Upland. I didn't like the feel of Central California the minute we arrived at Stephanie's little white clapboard house. The gray sky and humidity made me feel miles and miles from civilization, too isolated, everything so still and quiet, especially at night. The thrill of reuniting with Stephanie quickly turned into fear of being so far away from the Lances' house, which had become my home.

Stephanie and I walked around her family's property that first evening. Night—chilly and quiet—descended on us, and my heart began beating too fast. I felt uncomfortable and nervous.

The closer we got to bedtime, the more uneasy I felt. I said nothing. I was with Stephanie and her family. I knew them and loved them. *Everything is going to be okay*, I told myself.

Stephanie and her two sisters shared a bedroom outfitted with bunk beds. I crawled onto one of the top bunks. Janie, Stephanie, and Kimberly were all chattering and laughing, and although I was filled with anxiety, I did the same.

I thought I would be all right until Stephanie's mother came in to switch off the light. "Time to go to sleep," she cooed, and that's when the fear really kicked in. My heart pounded, and I felt like I could hardly breathe. Waves of panic washed over me.

Mother's not all right, I thought. *She's in trouble*. I rolled over on my stomach and punched up the pillow, turning my head one way, then the other, desperately trying to settle in. But my mind leapt from one terrifying thought to the next. *No one can reach you. Mother is hurt. Someone has hurt her. She's been stabbed, and no one can reach you.*

For my mother, the idea of adjusting to prison began by imagining the terror of someone knifing her through the curtain in the public shower rooms. While this never happened, her fears became my fears. I didn't know what the prison looked like because we still had not been able to visit Mom. Everything in front of me was unknown, unpredictable, and scary, while everything behind me felt surreal.

I wept, careful to do so quietly, so I wouldn't wake anyone.

I turned over on my back. I lay in the darkness regretting I'd ever come to Stephanie's, certain I was being punished for leaving my mother alone.

All night, I tossed and turned, had to go to the toilet, returned to bed to more tossing and turning, stumbled back to the toilet, and then to bed again, until at some early morning hour, exhausted, I finally drifted off to sleep.

In daylight, I no longer felt as afraid. I told Stephanie's mom about my turbulent night. She got right on the phone and called Mrs. Lance, who assured me that my mother was safe, nothing had happened to her, and she had Stephanie's phone number. I stayed a day or two more after that, and no more panic attacks ruined my sleep. But I was relieved to get back to the Lances and didn't want to go anywhere for a while.

Meanwhile, my mother resolved she was going to survive and not live in fear, which meant getting used to things that would have horrified her in her previous life. Finding a protector was key. This was not because she was a murderer. Nobody in prison gives a damn if you kill your spouse or how you do it. The mark against my mother was her social class. A woman married to a professional, living where we lived, a woman educated and accepted in society, was anathema to the other women in prison. Their first plan was to make sure you understood that your past life was going to be a liability for you now.

I started to visit my mother once a week, and those regular visits exposed me to a world unknown to most teenagers.

A tall, handsome pimp often visited his "girls" on the days I visited Mom. I got excited every time I'd see his brand-new, sparkling cream and chrome Excalibur with shiny brown rolled-leather seats taking up two parking spaces in the lot. He dressed to match his car: cream panama hat, double-breasted cream linen suit and silk shirt, an African American Jay Gatsby. He was at least six feet tall, a beautiful caramel color, hair conked, wearing aviator sunglasses. He was long and lanky, fingernails manicured, a gold pinky ring on his little finger. His shoulders and arms moved in time with his hips and legs, liquid and graceful. I was in love with him.

He knew I had a crush on him. I couldn't help staring at him, although I thought I was being discreet. When I did catch his eye behind those dark glasses, he grinned knowingly. I fantasized he was my lover, even though I had no idea what that meant. In my imagination, it all worked out well for me. I was his princess and the others were his prostitutes. At the same time, I was afraid of him.

One day, I pointed him out to Mom and revealed my secret crush.

"Just keep him a fantasy," she warned. "He's not going to mess with you anyway. He can read you a lot better than you can read him. You don't want to be slapped around, addicted to heroin, totally dependent on a man like that."

She went on to explain that pimps keep their girls happy while they serve their prison time by visiting them regularly and kissing heroin-filled balloons into their mouths.

For my part, I complained about everything and wanted everything I had been used to. Mom cried with me. My life was so different now that I had lost my family. Among other things, I had been used to an allowance. I had earned $4 or $5 a week cleaning up the kitchen, packing family lunches, and doing my own ironing. Now I didn't have spending money or the wardrobe I had been used to.

It wasn't that I was greedy. At fourteen, I didn't quite grasp we no longer had any money or that my mom was essentially powerless to provide for her children. We lost all but one of our life insurance policies because of her conviction. The remaining one was set up in a trust for us, which only the Lances had access to, and even then, extracting money was a struggle. Mom didn't understand money. She believed the trust fund provided her kids with whatever they wanted, which wasn't the case.

Still, she did her best even from within the prison walls. At Christmas, she asked my brothers and me to give her our lists. We knew to keep them short, and Mom always found a way to honor our wishes. A lot of people, but mostly Sandy, chipped in to help. We didn't understand at the time that we were all Mom cared about, her reason to live.

Soon enough, however, we found out that this was more self-centered than to do with motherly love. It had to do with survival. To become a kingpin in prison, she required her children to participate in that survival.

It started with mace, a spice related to the nutmeg seed that came in little metal tin cans available at any supermarket. It takes a lot of mace to get high, and most don't try it twice. But it's popular in prisons because other drugs are harder to get—or at least that was true during the years my mother was in prison.

I could be found at the grocery store on a given weekend cleaning out the seasoning section's cans of mace, feeling everyone in the store was looking at me and wondering what the hell I planned to do with all of it. A ritual ensued after buying the mace: I dumped each can out on a flat surface, packed it in plastic sandwich bags until it was the size of the cardboard cylinder inside a roll of toilet paper, then sealed it with scotch tape. Sometimes my instructions were to bury several bags in the trash can in the women's restroom off the waiting room and cover it all up with paper towels. An inmate whose job was to clean the restroom would then retrieve it. Other times, I stuffed a few bags in my peacoat, then one at a time, I removed the bags from my pockets and left them on the side of my chair next to Mom. She then surreptitiously shoved them up her vagina like jumbo tampons. I sat there white with fear. Eventually she tried to soothe me, saying, "They're gone."

While my brothers found their criminal activities on behalf of our mother hilarious and fun, I was indignant and furious about this expectation of smuggling.

As we grew older, her requirements multiplied. Once my brothers had their driver's licenses, they also became smugglers. Unlike me, they saw it as a big adventure and loved it. They were under twenty-one, but that didn't bother Mom. A new venture was to sell vodka, popular because it left no smell on the breath. Once my brothers obtained the vodka, they delivered what Mom needed but kept a bottle for themselves, to party with their friend Tim. They drank the vodka, lit up a joint, and blasted the radio in Tim's yellow Volkswagen Bug or my brother Guy's '60s-era Oldsmobile that one of my uncles had given him.

The whole business was complicated. One of the jobs a trustworthy inmate could secure was groundskeeper, which allowed working outside—mowing the lawns, tending plants and trees, and getting a great tan. It was this inmate who retrieved all those vodka bottles my brothers tucked around the edges of the prison grounds.

Near the end of her term, Mom became a groundskeeper, and she was so happy; she loved being outdoors, loved trees, flowers, and plants—and a tan.

Sandy, my brothers, and I shared the responsibility of trafficking the goods Mom needed to distinguish herself, to gain status within the prison. Although frightened and angry about it, I did my share of stashing vodka in bathroom trash cans and smuggling mace and baggies of Valium. I believed if I refused, she would tell me not to come to the prison anymore.

Although Mom quickly found these and other ways to protect herself and was never hurt by her fellow inmates, she suffered her share of cruelties from security guards. She was a vegetarian, and prisons don't take special orders from their inmates. Since most of the dishes served in prison contained beef, pork, or chicken, Mom had to be clever about getting her protein. Hard-boiled eggs were the easiest source, but the kitchen didn't make hard-boiled eggs readily available. That meant Mom had to buy off someone in the kitchen to sneak her the eggs. She told me she became quite adept at strolling through the prison compound with eggs and other edibles locked between her legs. After being busted several times for hiding such contraband in her cell, she was locked down in the pit, a freezing room with no windows and a mattress on the floor.

She was sentenced to the pit more than once in her seven years, always for something trivial, like breaking food rules. She never had to stay long but told me it was horrible spending even one night in there. On a particularly freezing night, she began screaming, "Will someone call the dog pound and find out the temperature in there and at least set this thermometer to that of dogs?" She told me her screaming actually worked. Someone turned up the heat.

Mom told me the guards always "fucked with you," never letting you forget who was in charge and where you were. I knew the workings of prison life long before documentaries or dramas portrayed it—what the prisoners had to do to keep from being raped, beaten up, ostracized, or murdered.

I spent that summer working in a job Bud Lance found for me, helping people who could not afford attorneys find one from a rotating list of pro bono lawyers. He was the president of the organization that did this work.

I instantly developed a crush on Bud. I had a knockout body in my teens, and I wanted desperately to be precocious but didn't know how. I had a pink voile dress with white polka dots, cut very low. Every time I knew Bud was coming in, I wore that dress. Thank God he never seemed to see me as anything more than a silly teenager.

I also learned to drive that summer in Harold's stick-shift silver Porsche. We lurched all the way down Carnelian, one of us humiliated and the other trying hard not to laugh. Worse, my then-boyfriend passed us in his yellow Firebird, laughing.

For the first few months, visiting Mom was the highlight of my week. It was summer and the days were hot, my bare skin sticking to the hot vinyl seats of the Lances' green Chevy station wagon, windows rolled down, my hair flying. We'd motor down Euclid Avenue, my chin resting on the open window, passing Squire's restaurant, where Sandy worked as a waitress during the summers. We'd pass J. J. Newberry's and the movie theater where Mom once dropped me off, insisting that if I wanted a bag of popcorn, I needed to get it myself. We rolled out of town past broken-down houses and abandoned barns, the dry earth fanning away from us until the Lances turned the station wagon left onto a windy road, taking us past dairy cows, a grassy ditch shadowing each side of the road, and then finally turning right, into the brick entrance of the prison.

Harold later recalled, "You'd gripe and complain about living with us, and rather than calm you down, try and make it easy for you, your mom would fire you up with the injustice of it all and return three angry and unhappy kids to us at the end of the hour."

I remembered how the drive home wasn't so carefree, how anger hung thick in the air, nothing like the ride down there. The Lances surely realized that someone needed to talk to my mother, set up some parameters, but there was no one who'd dare suggest to my mom—or to us, for that matter—that we change up what we were doing. The Lances never stopped taking us down there. They just paid the price, and so did we, week after week and year after year.

During the time we lived with the Lances, Guy and Ron frequently sought me out for succor in hopes I could change something. Their grievances were minor, having mostly to do with adjusting to a new style of being parented. The poor Lances tried, but all I saw was unfairness where there was none, inconsistencies that didn't exist, abuses that weren't happening. On behalf of my brothers, I lashed out with the fury of a mother protecting her cubs. I cried with my brothers and seethed with anger because I was washed in guilt for leaving them alone while I was at school.

I remember raging first at Joan and then, after she abruptly left the room to fetch Harold, continuing to scream about what a spoiled brat their youngest daughter, Julia, was. Harold just pulled me to him. I sobbed and sobbed while he stood there awkwardly, trying to calm me down and comfort me as Julia listened at the bottom of the staircase.

Julia became a lawyer. We Millers became drug addicts. I don't think we gave that family a moment's peace.

My brothers and I lived with the Lances for about four years, beginning in the spring of 1965. During the summer of 1965, the Lances bought a new home on Carnelian, one block down from Bella Vista. They reclaimed my bedroom furniture, and I had my own downstairs bedroom with a bathroom right around the corner. A barn sat behind the house, and a swimming pool glistened in the sunlight on the back patio. The Lances bought two horses, a mean white and brown Shetland pony and a mare. There also were cats, dogs, and several banty chickens I disliked. I took to carrying a shovel with me when I walked to the barn so that when those stupid chickens ran to greet me with a peck, I swung the shovel as hard as I could at those little beasts, knocking the air out of them but not killing them.

In reality, the Lances were a perfect fit for me, better than my own parents. They were easygoing, loved to read and left books all over the place, so I never felt in want of something to read. I read *Atlas Shrugged* and other Ayn Rand books and J. D. Salinger's *The Catcher in the Rye*. The Lances were carnivores, which suited me. A field of clovers ran next to our house. While my brother Ron rode that wicked little Shetland pony, who often tried to buck the rider, I rode the mare. The one advantage of Ron's pony was that he was fast, so the rider was guaranteed, if you stayed on him, to win a race across the clover field.

The Lances also owned a cabin in Big Bear. The truth was that life was never better for the Miller children, but we did not show gratitude. Instead, we were critical and sulky. Unlike the pretenses Mom tried to keep up with cleanliness and order, the Lances were messy, something that drove me crazy. I didn't understand at the time that homes without fear and anger, homes with lots of pets, homes that encouraged your predilections, were messy homes, but in healthy ways. In the end, to save what was left of their once-happy home, the Lances more or less kicked us all out. I spent most of my life during that time looking for a family and didn't find a home and family for another twenty years.

CHAPTER 21:

Appeals

My mom's attorneys began appealing to the higher courts immediately after her conviction and her arrival at CIW (California Institution for Women). Until her release from prison after seven years, I lived in a cycle of hope and despair. When one appeal was denied, I felt reassured that the next appeal to a higher court had a much more likely chance of being granted, and hope would buck me up again.

My mom was not someone to get on her knees and pray. If someone was going to change her circumstance, he or she was going to be flesh and blood, not God. Her original defense team petitioned the California courts for a new trial on the grounds that her civil rights had been denied in several instances. All of the lower courts disagreed and did not grant her a new trial.

One day in prison, Mom read an article about F. Lee Bailey, prominently known then, and later for his part in the O. J. Simpson trial. In the article, Bailey criticized prosecutors. Mom wrote a letter to her father about the article, asking him to seek out Bailey. When my grandmother read the letter, she contacted a friend she believed might be able to help. The friend got in touch with Bailey and told him about Mom's failed petitions to the lower courts arguing that her civil rights had been denied. He agreed to represent her appeal to the US Supreme Court, as did well-known attorneys Robert Steinberg and Alan Dershowitz.

Bailey was perfect for my mom. They both had a bad attitude toward the justice system.

Her petition made its way to the US Supreme Court and ended up being argued by Dershowitz. The petition for a new trial rested on five issues. Only two argued that Mom's constitutional rights were denied, and since those justified a new trial, they stood out to me as most important.

The first of these two involved an informant. "Undercover agent . . . Peggy Fisk, not a real prisoner, [was] planted in [Mom's] cell . . ." and urged her to turn against her attorneys and "throw herself on the alleged mercy" of Sheriff Bland without revealing who she really was or advising Mom of her right to remain silent. The Supreme Court rejected the argument, contending that Ed Foley should have objected to Peggy Fisk before she ever took the stand and that his cross-examination of Peggy Fisk bolstered his defense, not the prosecution's, and didn't hurt Mom.

The second issue was "whether it is unconstitutional for a prosecutor, who does not [really] inten[d] to seek the death penalty from the jury, to disqualify for cause those jurors who have conscience scruples against the death penalty."

In other words, did prosecutor Don Turner err in Mom's case by questioning their qualms about the death penalty and only selecting those who did not object to it? He did not explain why, but it became clear he didn't want jurors who were against the death penalty. Turner never intended to ask for the death penalty, but he wanted jurors who supported it. These jurors were more likely to convict.

In my mother's appeal to the Supreme Court of the United States, October Term 1966, *Lucille Miller v. State of California*, her lawyers argued: "It has been widely recognized that jurors who do not oppose the death penalty frequently have many other characteristics relevant in the trial of a criminal case. Prosecutors are well aware of this and consequently favor such jurors—even when they are not seeking the imposition of capital punishment—over those who oppose the death penalty."

The Supreme Court did not find in my mother's favor on this point, again stating that her attorney neglected to "object to the prospective jurors" who indicated they supported capital punishment.

While the Supreme Court agreed to hear these arguments, it too eventually declined to grant her a new trial, allowing the lower courts' decisions to stand.

In the two issues I detail, all of the courts cite my mom's defense team as the problem. In my adult years, I had more than one boyfriend who was an attorney, and I heard on multiple occasions from people who'd studied my mother's case in law school as an example of what not to do on a defense team.

CHAPTER 22:

Rio Lindo Academy

After my mother's trial, I wanted to go away to boarding school to finish my junior and senior years in high school. I was going to have to change schools anyway because the Adventist school I attended only went through tenth grade. While I had given up God, I had not given up Adventism, because I needed the familiarity it offered. Rio Lindo Academy was in Healdsburg, California, some ten hours north of Southern California, and I thought it would offer me some anonymity from the exposure I felt in the aftermath of my mother's case.

The Lances drove me to Healdsburg, starting a tradition of driving up the coast on Highway 101, stopping at the Madonna Inn in San Luis Obispo for lunch. This became a routine during the years I drove back and forth between Northern and Southern California. Even though the inn was much closer to Los Angeles than to Sonoma County, it marked a transition for me from one life to another. A cross between a Tudor mansion and the witch's cottage in "Hansel and Gretel," the famous inn beckoned to travelers. It was like stepping into a storybook with its pink and green rose-printed carpet, gleaming copper dining tables and chairs, and chunky ruby, pink, and sapphire goblets. While we never stayed overnight, I always wanted to. Each room was decorated in a different theme. The room styled to look like a cave and the one covered in zebra skins caught my imagination.

After lunch, I loved browsing in the gift shop, where every sparkling item from the restaurant was available for purchase. The inn was like stepping through the looking glass. Colors sparkled. Surfaces gleamed. I walked on roses, even if it was just the print of the carpet. Outside, I could barely stand my world. But the Madonna Inn was magical. Even when I had to leave, everything was different, better, lusher, and more beautiful the farther north we went.

Healdsburg was destined to become an expensive and fashionable little town tucked into a valley of wineries, but in the '60s, it was a dumpy, dried-up little town in rural Sonoma County. Santa Rosa was the closest town to Healdsburg that offered anything to do.

When I attended the school, the student body numbered under three hundred. The boys' brick dorm occupied one end of the campus and the girls' the other end. Between were the chapel, classrooms, and cafeteria. The Russian River ran parallel to the campus, too far back to see from there, but it was a short hike down through trees and shrubbery.

I did not know who my roommate was going to be except that she was a senior and her name was Linda. I thought it was weird that a senior was willing to room with someone she didn't know. This made me think she was unpopular.

Probably the truth was that Linda was asked to room with me because she was a friendly, nice young woman, willing to look after this "special" student. And that's exactly what she did. Linda was already set up in our room when I arrived. It was a Friday. She was a bubbly, petite brunette who eagerly welcomed me but at the same time announced her parents were coming to get her to spend the weekend before school started in San Francisco. I could have started crying then and there. Linda was so nice. I needed her. It scared me that I was going to have to spend my first weekend at Rio Lindo alone.

Immediately and unfairly, I felt angry at the Lances. This was another one of their blunders, their inability to get it, to know the proper etiquette and ritual for dropping a teenager off at boarding school. I did not consider that Mrs. Lance had tried to pull a nice wardrobe together for me, shopped for all the bedding and personal supplies she imagined I needed, that both Harold and Joan Lance had bundled this angry, sulking teenager into their station wagon and had begun the Madonna Inn tradition. I was nothing but critical. Yet I was devastated when they pulled away in their green Chevy wagon.

My parents would have gotten this right, I thought angrily as I watched them drive away. I wished for my mother, her style making sure I arrived with the most abundant and beautiful wardrobe, tending to every detail of my room, perhaps hanging cute little flowered curtains, bedspreads and shams to match. Whisking me off for lunch at the most fashionable restaurant in Healdsburg (even though there were none).

My resentment didn't end there.

How nice could Linda really be, I thought of my new roommate, *if she could leave me alone like this?*

There must have been plenty of other kids whose parents hadn't swept them away for a fun-filled weekend. Going to the cafeteria alone was unthinkable, same with the bathroom and showers, both of which were down the hall and public, not private. But in memory I saw no one, didn't eat, and never bathed or used the bathroom. I just cried.

I do remember the joy I felt when Linda returned. She took care of me, introducing me around and walking with me to class

As it turned out, Linda and I didn't have anything in common. She was a good student, held a student body office, and had Rick, her steady boyfriend, whom she married after college. Kathy, the girl who lived in the room next door, became my best friend. She too was serious about student life at Rio, and she too met her future husband, David, there. I adored Kathy, a petite blonde with a short pixie haircut and an endless good mood. We stirred up so much fun together and became roommates our senior year.

But Kathy was grounded, and I wasn't. She had a beautiful soprano voice and sang in the choir, often singing solos. My singing career had been cut short after my third lesson because of my mother's arrest. And while Kathy found it helpful to study for her exams, I preferred using this time to read long novels such as Margaret Mitchell's *Gone with the Wind.* I always had my nose in a book but never a book for one of my classes. I didn't take college prep courses. Geometry and chemistry scared me. I took French for one year. The teacher gave us an aptitude test for languages, and I scored high but earned a D in the class. Being told I had an aptitude for French made me think I didn't have to do anything to get an A. In my mom's letters to Sandy, she was constantly fretting about my bad grades—an F in history, a D in French.

I liked English but couldn't retain anything I read. I just couldn't concentrate. I needed distractions. I wish I'd immersed myself in my schoolwork, cared about grades as I once had, but I was too crushed to focus. Also, my English teacher was disconcerting, with his bad breath and scar from cleft-palate surgery. He seemed to take special interest in my appearance. He kept staring at me in class. One day, he announced that he needed to see me in his office, a little glass cubicle in the classroom. Furious, I followed him, leaving behind the rest of the class to speculate on what I had done wrong. Everyone in the class could see what was going on, though they couldn't hear anything. He pulled two straight-back chairs from the wall and sat them face to face, positioned his chair too close to mine, and leaned toward me, his foul breath a distraction, scolding, "You're wearing too much makeup."

Christ, I thought to myself, *he's halted an entire English class for this?*

Outraged, I replied, "I am not wearing makeup."

"Yes, you are," he insisted.

"Where?" I asked.

"You're wearing eyebrow pencil," he said as he raised his index finger to sweep across my eyebrow.

I leaned back. "Those are my eyebrows. Why would I use eyebrow pencil when my eyebrows are already so much darker than my hair?"

"Well, I don't know, but it sure looks like eyebrow pencil to me," he replied, less sure of himself now.

"Well, it's not," I insisted.

Silence.

The only class I was good at and enjoyed was typing. I liked the teacher, a tall, thin woman who always wore black patent flats, which I figured was because she was taller than her husband. I wasn't the best in typing class, but I was good, and it has served me well.

Secretly, I liked my home economics class. It was considered cheesy, though, so I kept my enjoyment to myself, which meant not making much of an effort.

I was a little bit of everybody and no one in particular. My favorite people to hang with were in the wilder crowds.

Sneaking to the river after church, stripping down to our bikinis, often bringing a picnic, my girlfriends and I hid every time we heard the art teacher's motorcycle slamming through the brush in search of sinners, whom he never found because we knew where to hide. These incidents were my distractions. I was the second-best sprinter in the school. I didn't care. My coach saw promise in me, but I was lazy, not interested in being the best. My depression kept me exhausted all the time, and then, it did not occur to me that I might be depressed. I just missed my mom and my brothers, my family. I cried frequently.

No one at Rio Lindo revealed they knew about my mother or my past. I didn't talk about it, either. I felt out of place and empty when my friends' parents came to visit them on weekends or when a mother-daughter banquet left me alone or adopted by a friend's mother. I never invited Joan Lance or even let her know of these events. I did not understand then how sensitive the faculty and staff of Rio Lindo Academy were to my situation, but in retrospect, I came to understand that they, like so many others in my life, were deeply attuned to what I was going through.

My guardian angel—who to me was the devil—during these years was the headmistress of the girls' dormitory, Mrs. Pluhvoy, who quietly watched over me. I considered her a nuisance and never responded to her kindness. She held me accountable for pranks, like removing all the doorknobs from the dorm rooms. I didn't care if they kicked me out. But I recognized that Mrs. Pluhvoy intended to keep me at Rio, and later when she became the dean at Pacific Union College, where I attended my first years of college, she did her best to keep me from being dismissed.

I always had a boyfriend, but my attractions sometimes included boys with girlfriends. The one boy I always wanted at Rio Lindo Academy was Peter, tall, with blue eyes and a full and beautiful mouth. He was handsome, funny, and clever. Peter was a year behind me and lived in Sacramento. I never became as important to Peter as he was to me. We were good friends. I managed to be his date on one of the school's canoe trips, but never his girlfriend.

I was thin but big breasted, which embarrassed me. By the time of my crush on Peter, I had only kissed one boy on the Lances' front porch, and he wore braces. While my passions simmered, I had no idea what to do with them. The confusing thing for boys was that I was considered wild. I loved to sneak off to the Russian River and smoke cigarettes, swore like a sailor even at sixteen, and hated adults. But when it came to boys, I was a prude.

One time, I used my attractiveness to get what I wanted from a boy. Danny was a jock who really strutted his stuff. He wasn't my type or in my crowd, but we became a couple for a brief period. He was a decent guy destined to be a physical education teacher, but he soon grew bored with me, and we broke up. This was right around the time of Rio Lindo's senior prom. I hadn't considered that I might not have a date. That did happen; no one asked me to the prom. By this time, Danny was dating a friend of mine, Pam. When it became clear that no one was going to ask me to the prom, I panicked. I knew Danny still liked me, so I stole him back from Pam, who graciously released him from being her prom date, wanting him to be with the girl he liked best.

In a religion where everything—including dancing, wearing makeup or jewelry, and eating meat—is a sin, a senior prom wasn't much. Our prom consisted of a vegetarian dinner served in the school cafeteria, decorated with a few balloons and a few banners with things like SENIOR PROM CLASS OF '68 printed on them. A table stood at the front of the room for all the officers and their dates. Round tables fanned out from the head table to accommodate the rest of the seniors, maybe fifty kids. Nobody at Rio bought a prom dress. We just wore one of our nicest church dresses. Mine was one my mother had a fellow inmate make, a loosely knitted pink dress that clung to my body and had a deeply scooped neckline revealing my D cup cleavage. I'm surprised I wasn't sent back to my dorm room to change, but maybe my obvious self-consciousness and awkwardness seemed punishment enough.

Had I been a different kind of teenager, I might have been the belle of the ball. Instead, I did everything I could to hide myself all that night, hunching my shoulders and endlessly shifting the dress up and down and from left to right, an indication of the many conflicting feelings with which I was struggling.

Pam sat at the table of dateless coeds while I joined Danny at the class officers' table. This backstabbing grab to be Danny's date had occurred within hours of the event. Speeches for the evening were already written, plans for the evening completed. Everyone knew Danny should have walked in with Pam. That he walked in with me took the breath out of the room. I pretended to ignore the gasp as I sauntered to the head table to take my place beside my date, but I felt sick to my stomach.

It only got worse when all the jokes from the speeches that evening were references to Pam and Danny. The entire evening was a bust.

At some point, I looked over at Pam's table. She was laughing and whispering to the other girls, having plenty of fun, a lot more than I was having. I needed the evening to end. Both of us knew that I should be sitting where Pam was and that Pam should be sitting with Danny.

CHAPTER 23:

Mom's Demands

By the time I came home the summer between my junior and senior year at Rio Lindo, I had a driver's license and no longer needed anyone to taxi me. My mother told Sandy that now that I had my license, my brothers and I could take over the job of smuggling contraband. We did not look like traffickers. We were well-mannered and clean-cut kids. All the officers working the front were nice to us and never searched us. I guess they couldn't fathom a mother expecting her teenage children to supply contraband so that their mother wouldn't kill herself or try to escape, which were the reasons she used to manipulate us.

My favorite guard was a young woman who always wore bright-orange lipstick and orange nail polish, her hands tiny and feminine as she handed me the clipboard to sign in. She once told me she was a probation officer, which sounded less intimidating to me than being a prison guard. I wasn't just afraid of sneaking stuff to my mom. I felt guilty that I was betraying people at the front desk who were so kind to us.

But Mom felt no guilt compromising her children. She felt we owed her.

My main job during this time was smuggling in Lancôme. Mother insisted her skin was just too delicate for the cheap creams they sold at the prison commissary. Her solution to my fuss over smuggling liquor and mace was to promote me to smuggling the expensive face cream. It didn't matter to her that I hadn't seen her for three months because I'd been away at school. Once she knew I was coming to visit, I was given a job to do.

Her friends bought the Lancôme and turned it over to me.

On the day of my first visit after I got back from school, Mom stepped forward to greet me, wearing a prison regulation cotton skirt and shell. Placing her manicured hands on my shoulders, she pulled me to her in a flimsy hug, whispering in my ear, "Did you bring them?"

"Yes," I hissed in return, my body stiffening.

Mom ignored my resistance. "Which pocket?"

"Left," I responded.

Having settled this, she guided me to sit on her right side.

God, I hated this. All I could think about was what would happen if I got caught.

"Get our Snickers out of the machine," she said. "You can give me the stuff when you come back and hand me the candy."

When I handed over the goods, my mother, in the blink of an eye, shifted her body from one hip to the other, lifting a butt cheek as she slid two lipsticks and a tube of cream right up her vagina. At this audacious and bewildering moment, my life hung in the balance between my continued freedom or joining my mother in lockup. I never, no matter how hard I tried, figured out how she performed this magical disappearing act so swiftly and smoothly. I never, in seven years, actually saw it happen.

"There. Gone," she assured me.

"How do you do that?" I asked, my breathing returning, my shoulders relaxing as I could finally settle into our visit, safe one more time.

This is how it went every time for seven years. Sometimes my smuggling worked another way that was more comfortable for me. I carried the cosmetics in my purse. Even though it required more stealth on my part, I was less afraid. If the guard did happen to check my purse, carrying makeup or skin care products wouldn't look out of place. When I was carrying the goods this way, I cautiously removed them and laid them beside me. When I rose to go to the candy machine, my mom disappeared the loot.

Each time I returned from the machines, I wished this would be my last undercover job. All I wanted was to sit beside Mom and spill out my troubles, troubles she mostly couldn't fix, but sometimes, when it came to my material or financial woes, like wanting a new pair of shoes or some extra cash, she made it happen. Within a few days, Sandy or some other friend of Mom's would pick me up, take me to lunch, and hand me whatever it was I had desired.

I wasn't making requests on a regular basis, but I did use my mom when I felt at my wit's end. She was great at giving advice about boyfriends, although there wasn't much advice to give me because I was so puritanical. She'd convinced the Lances to give me a lot of freedom, leading to going away to boarding school. My brothers left Adventist schools once they entered high school and left the Lances, moving from friend to friend's homes, until at sixteen Ron was living in an apartment of his own.

Mom couldn't live with me, but she saw to it I didn't have to live very long with someone else. We were scattered, yet I longed for the day when we could live with her again, Guy, Ron, and me. Kimi now lived with my grandparents.

CHAPTER 24:

Pacific Union College

Two roads leaving Napa run toward St. Helena—Highway 29 and the Silverado Trail, which is faster but scary at night. Highway 29 becomes Main Street in St. Helena and passes the Christian Brothers Winery, standing like a medieval abbey. Then it becomes Deer Park Road, which in turn becomes Howell Mountain Road and winds eight miles up to Pacific Union College, owned by Seventh-day Adventists and nestled in an idyllic mountain setting rich in ponderosa pine and Douglas fir. I never paid much attention to the educational value Pacific Union College offered its students, but I did relish that it was a lovers' paradise, perfect for walks, picnics, and secret drinking parties.

I attended PUC because there was nowhere else for me to go. I only moved on to college because that was what most of my classmates from Rio Lindo Academy were doing. I had no ambition or any idea of what I wanted to be or to do with my life. Students from the homes of doctors and nurses tended to follow in their parents' footsteps. None of that held any attraction for me. I knew I had no discipline for the sciences.

Again, I arrived without a roommate. I was placed with Candy, and we roomed together our freshman year. She was everything I was not, including being the youngest of three of a prominent family in Lodi, California. Candy planned on being a nurse. She was always generous with me, in a casual way, not stuck up, though she had the air of a person who'd grown up with affluence, where the extra family car is a Porsche or a BMW, and that's totally normal.

I envied Candy and fantasized about having a life like hers—with a beautiful house to go home to, a fabulous wardrobe, fancy vacations, chic and elegant parents. But that was a fantasy, too, because my family would never have had the affluence and respectability of hers. We'd been in tatters since the day I was born.

Like most freshmen, I changed roommates the following year. There was never a fallout between Candy and me; we were just not the same. Candy was studious; I was not. Candy didn't smoke; I did. Candy didn't run in a ramble-scramble crowd; I did. Candy never got in trouble; I did.

I spent a lot of time my freshman year with Gary. He was a junior premed student, the best catch on campus. I knew him from the basketball team because I attended the games. He was a clean-cut intellectual, hair neatly trimmed, who wore Clark Kent black-rimmed glasses, an athlete who played his heart out on a crummy small college basketball team. He didn't seem my type, nor me his. I had no major, earned mostly Cs, and was a slacker who preferred smoking cigarettes, getting drunk, and swearing. When his best friend's girlfriend, Suzanne, knocked on my door one Friday night to ask on Gary's behalf if I would be his date at the Warriors' basketball game the next night, I was surprised and flattered.

And on that first date, chemistry radiated between us. It truly was love at first sight. Who knew two such different people could be attracted to each other?

From the beginning, Gary's parents disapproved. They discouraged their only son from getting involved with me. They did not want him dating a girl whose mother was in prison for murdering her husband. He came from a prominent family in a small community. It wouldn't look good for him to be with me. They pleaded with him and ultimately threatened to cut off his spending money and take his car if he didn't break up with me. Their threats never worked for long.

I didn't fit in with Gary's friends. I had nothing to talk about with them. I wasn't going to play a game of softball or touch football. Gary didn't fit in with my friends, either, nor did he want to, especially not with Peter. My close friendship with him drove Gary crazy. While Gary studied in the library, I played with Peter and my roommate Donna. Unfortunately, his studiousness failed to rub off on me. We both had something the other one wanted, which kept us together—off and on—for many years. Because of my trauma, I was attracted to Gary, who had a settled and conventional life, and Gary was attracted to me because of his conventional life. A powerful physical attraction augmented the intensity.

While I had limited experience with boys, Gary had no experience with girls.

One afternoon, about a year after we'd first started dating, we parked by the side of the road and hiked to an abandoned winery my friends and I had discovered, a place with tall grass and brush surrounding a crumbling two-story brick winery with a small creek running quietly beside it. I asked Gary to explore the winery with me.

It had a half-rotted stairway that led to a small area on the second floor. An arched window with a ledge jutting out let us marvel at the expanse of valley before us. Then we climbed back down to sit by the creek.

Gary began kissing me.

I pulled away slightly and took a breath. "Can I ask you a question?"

"Sure," he replied.

I shifted my weight. Let a beat pass. "Have you ever French-kissed a girl?"

Relief melted over his face. He kind of grinned. Looking straight at me, he replied, "No, I haven't."

I smiled back. "Would you like to learn?" I asked.

The answer was in the gesture.

Gary was a fast learner on matters of love and on everything else. We first made love on the ledge of the winery about a week later. We both were virgins. I was nineteen. He was twenty.

After our first time together, everything for Gary and me was about sex. We snuck off every chance we got. As long as we were alone, exploring each other's bodies, everything was perfect, the world beautiful. And in this valley there were plenty of places to do that. We drove. We hiked. We walked. We made love. We laughed and enjoyed ourselves.

I once fell in a creek on one of our walks. Gary realized I wasn't behind him and turned around to see water swirling around my chest. I had slipped on a boulder as I crossed the creek. We both thought this was hilarious. I was soaking wet as we tramped back to campus.

By the time Gary graduated from college and entered medical school in Southern California, we'd broken up and come back together many times.

I wanted to marry Gary, but the trajectory of my life was so different from his. As much as I tried to convince

Gary and myself that I could change and enter his world, I understood that I couldn't remake myself. I wasn't religious, lacked any interest in Adventism, and no longer believed in God. I wanted to drink, smoke cigarettes and pot, and pop black beauties (Dexedrine) and cross tops (Benzedrine), because the effect of amphetamines gave me a false sense of control. I wanted to run free and naked with my best friends. I was both free-spirited and self-destructive, hiding from the stark reality of my life.

CHAPTER 25:

Self-Destructing

Much of my early college behavior was dictated by depression. Yet one aspect of college life offered relief—the beauty of Napa Valley. Nature invited me in and created a sense of wonderment that could set aside my sorrows. St. Helena was a very different place in the late 1960s and early '70s than it would become in later years, a tourist destination with its gourmet restaurants, lavish hotels, and elegant wineries. Donna and Peter and I thought the entire valley belonged to us. Its glory was its lush sweeping hills during spring, the creeks, the woods, the deserted wineries and endless trails carving their way through thick brush and trees, winding through green rolling hills, quiet except for nature's whispers. These were private estates owned by city dwellers, not easy to find.

Our secrets included several magnificent hideaways. None was as hard to reach or offered such a spectacular reward as one particular spot we loved. Walking for what seemed like forever along a dirt road too narrow for a vehicle but wider than a trail, we were guided to its opening by the sun; our secret place was breathtaking. We climbed over a flimsy fence and raced to the top of the hill, stripped off our clothes, pulled out bread and salami, unscrewed our cheap wine that we'd stolen from Safeway, and spent the afternoon gamboling, drinking, and dancing, frolicking trespassers, a debauched communing with God.

Sometimes we picnicked in yet another lush setting in the valley. One time Peter wandered off. We found him naked, examining the leaves on the branches of a tree.

"He thinks he's Adam," I noted.

Although I was in love with both Donna and Peter, these picnics never became sexual. They never knew my desire to melt into both of them.

During my sophomore year and until I left my junior year, I roomed with Donna. We occupied the best and biggest room on the third floor of our dorm. Everything—the way we dressed, the way we decorated our dorm room with tie-dye and macramé—screamed hippie. We had a blast during that year and a half. She lived in Sacramento and introduced me to her friends from there, including Peter. These were my people: students, smokers, drinkers, and drug users who sometimes enjoyed escaping reality. I needed to escape reality.

Sometimes we fancied being outlaws, which suited me because I didn't care if I went to jail. We liked to pair up and shoplift small stuff in local shops in St. Helena. We met up later to display our wares, a kind of contest. I loved the adrenaline of the fear of getting caught and the thrill of getting away with it.

Donna and I, along with our friend Dolly, were finally caught and arrested for stealing sunglasses in a department store in Sacramento. My two girlfriends were terrified. I was not. The cops were kind enough to suggest that we throw away anything in our purses that might get us into more trouble.

We were booked. Our friend Dolly hadn't stolen anything. We explained this to the cops, that she was innocent and shouldn't be charged; they agreed. Donna wanted to call her boyfriend to bail us out, but I was willing to spend the night in jail—a kind of testimony to my mother. None of this was as scary as trafficking contraband to my mother when I was fifteen. I had disdain for the police. I figured if my mother could make it through multiple years in prison, I could certainly spend a night in jail.

My girlfriends were also terrified about their parents finding out. I didn't care who found out. I was self-destructive and fearless about what might happen to me.

In the end, friends bailed us out. Then I called Harold Lance. We were right on the cusp of being charged as either juveniles or adults. To be charged as adults could leave a black spot on our records. If charged as juveniles, we could serve a short probation and have our records expunged. Harold contacted a lawyer in Sacramento, an expert on our situation. When I learned the difference, I wanted my record expunged.

The fee was $1,400, which Harold paid, but he made me pay him back with the money I made over the summer working as a receptionist in a medical building.

Our friends and boyfriends showed up in court and did not behave well, laughing and smacking their hands together when they found something funny. Harold Lance called me that night.

"Debbie, you and your friends cannot be disrespectful in the courtroom. If it continues, the judge will charge you as adults, and that's something you don't want to happen." This chastened me. While this was a good lesson, I stole a ring one more time to assure myself I hadn't lost my touch.

Gary was away at medical school, so I was surprised to see him one day as I was coming out of Safeway with Donna. I had just bought a pack of cigarettes and was about to light up when I saw Gary climbing out of his car. I'd promised to change, but I hadn't; in fact, I hadn't changed a thing.

I pulled out my cigarettes. "Hold these for me," I said to Donna. I took off running toward Gary, who wasn't running toward me.

I wrapped myself around him and gave him a big kiss on the lips. He didn't kiss me back. His only response to my exuberance was to grab me as though to keep us both from falling.

He'd never been so cold. I watched his lips moving, saw the seriousness on his face, but his voice seemed far away. He told me he was leaving me for good and had driven to St. Helena to tell me.

My jaw locked. My tongue thickened. This couldn't be true. I didn't believe him. *He's been pressured into this again*, I thought.

"Gary," I managed to force myself to say, "do you still love me?"

He answered, "No."

I asked him again for good measure.

Adamant, he stiffly repeated, "No."

I stood frozen in front of him, so far away and unable to respond. I didn't cry. I didn't beg. I turned around and walked back to Donna and attended my cooking class that afternoon.

I never mentioned Gary's name again, just as I never talked about my mother. When too much time had passed, friends told me he asked about me, asked if I had spoken of him; they told him, truthfully, that I never mentioned his name.

I had lost my love, and I didn't know how to communicate that I cared about him.

In the face of everyone I loved leaving me, my defense strategy was to roll up inside myself and never show that I was hurt.

Before my mother's arrest and trial, I had been a good student. In my heart, I still wanted that. With Gary gone, I tried to focus on school. I decided that if I planted myself in a library carrel every day, focused and studied, I'd become a new Debra.

One Monday morning during my sophomore year, I found a table in the library, determined to study. Several tables down from me sat Gerhard, a tall blond with long hair and a fabulous gold mustache. He looked about ten years older than I was. Gerhard was a senior. He had been studying for hours when I arrived. He was a poet. That afternoon, as he was leaving the library, he dropped onto the table where I sat a folded piece of paper, a poem he'd written. The poems continued, and soon we began chatting. I developed a crush on him immediately.

I started arriving at the library just minutes before Gerhard finished studying, which meant my studying never started.

As our relationship progressed, we drove into San Francisco to see plays. I listened to Gerhard discuss poetry and philosophy. I decided, with nothing to show for it, that I had turned into an intellectual. He continued to write me poetry. We drove to Southern California for the Rose Bowl parade. We arrived to stake our spot around ten at night. It was cold. It rained. We huddled close together and tried to sleep. By the time the parade started the next day, I couldn't have cared less about it. I was hungry and exhausted and needed a ladies' room.

That experience marked the end of my poet and me. It was the idea of him I had found attractive, not him. I liked being seen with him, tall and handsome in a Nordic way. I liked being tucked under his arm or strolling hand in hand down the street. People stared at us.

But it wasn't a passionate relationship. We never kissed or made love. The poet's life was too uncomfortable. I realized he was just a distraction from Gary. The poet was too serious. There wasn't any chemistry.

End of poet.

The only classes I studied for were psychology classes. I was appalled to learn about the Milgram study, the infamous Yale experiment demonstrating how people respond to authority by carrying out orders to shock other human beings for giving wrong answers. In my religion class, I enjoyed studying existentialism and chose it as the subject for my final essay. But I soon realized I knew next to nothing about existentialism, even though I enjoyed the lectures. I had no intentions of studying up on it, so I employed my friend Dennis to write the paper for me. I foolishly turned it in.

The next thing I knew, I was being hauled into the professor's office. I hated this professor because one day in class and apropos of nothing, he'd announced that God only approved of the missionary position in sex. I found him pointed and ugly, his wife plain. I tried to imagine them having sex.

"I'm afraid, young lady, you didn't write this paper," he accused. "What I want to know is who wrote it, because it's a very good paper."

I insisted I had written it.

"Your grade or participation in this class doesn't represent that you could write this kind of paper," he said.

"Well, I did write it," I said again.

His accusations and my denials continued for a few minutes. I would not back down. I knew a consequence awaited me, but I was going to accept that consequence without admitting anything. I would not take Dennis down with me, and I wasn't going to give my professor the satisfaction of a confession.

Finally, he said, "This is what I'm going to do about it. If you're going to insist that you wrote this paper, I'm giving it a D. Is that okay with you?"

I readily agreed. This was infinitely better than going through the hassle of what admitting to a plagiarized paper would mean.

I had zero guilt over that paper or any other unacceptable methods I used to get through all the colleges I attended before I finally graduated. I was broken, my circumstances chaotic. I wanted a college degree. When I felt incapable of succeeding, I cheated.

One paper for my freshman English class I wrote myself, putting hard work and thought into it. We were assigned to read Tennessee Williams's *The Glass Menagerie* and to write a paper on its theme, which we were to determine on our own. With pride and high expectations, I turned it in, eager for recognition I deserved. When the professor returned my essay, another "D" stared at me, along with a nasty note about how insulted he felt that I had thrown together such a mess of a paper. Devastated, I quietly tucked my failed masterpiece into my notes so that no one would notice my grade as I tried to stop the tears welling up. The message came loud and clear: I couldn't think and I couldn't write. I wasn't smart enough to understand literature, much less write about it or any other subject. The D I got on that paper in college turned out to be a defining moment. I allowed that grade to wipe out what little confidence I had in myself as a student.

CHAPTER 26:

Misfit

Once Gary broke up with me, there was nothing holding me back, no reason now to clean up my act. The first time my drinking affected others badly also was the first time I drank myself into a blackout. I didn't understand what a blackout was. I didn't know that people drove in blackouts, talked to other people, even had sex. I didn't know the bad thing about a blackout meant you functioned but without any conscious knowledge or control of your words or actions.

One Saturday afternoon during my junior year, I joined Donna and Dennis and some other classmates I didn't know, including a guy named Gabe, supposedly my date, to experience the delight of climbing a particular tree. It stood in the middle of a cleared area. Its trunk and branches were thick. The bottom branches dropped close to the ground, making it easy to climb. I stepped into Dennis's cupped palms while he hoisted me up to the first branch. Balancing my wine glass in one hand, I used my other arm to help sling myself over the tree's broad limb, settling on it as you would a horse.

I felt separate. Everyone else seemed to be happily sharing a partner. From my perch, the scene didn't appeal to me. I looked at my date, standing on the ground, a stocky, good-looking guy, brown hair dropping below his brow. He had kept trying to put his arm around me in the back seat of the car. I knew he had a girlfriend, and I didn't care. With my legs swinging, as though I could make that branch gallop away, I watched him in disgust. I don't know why I was his date, except that I partied and his girlfriend didn't. How had I ended up here? Half the people I didn't even know very well. This crowd was too subdued and self-conscious. I had been invited along for some reason that didn't sit right with me, that was turning out all wrong.

I leaned over and held out my glass. Dennis poured some more wine. It occurred to me I might be drinking more than anybody else. I felt angry about the entire afternoon.

It was dark when we rolled back to campus, and I went straight to bed.

The next thing I knew, it was morning and Donna was unusually quiet. I dressed and stumbled over to the cafeteria for breakfast. Gabe and his girlfriend sat at a table for two. I had the bad idea when I passed their table to stop and make a comment about the previous afternoon. Gabe glared at me. His girlfriend glared at me.

I felt dizzy. My head ached. I moved on to a table far from them. My mouth felt dry as I choked down scrambled eggs and toast. When I returned to my room, I told Donna that I hoped I hadn't embarrassed Gabe and his girlfriend. Donna remained silent.

"What's wrong with everybody?" I asked.

"Don't you remember what you said, how you treated Gabe last night?" she replied.

I couldn't remember a thing.

"Whatever kind of jerk he is, he didn't deserve the wrath

you threw at him. None of us could shut you up. It was embarrassing for everyone, especially Gabe."

Then she rolled out yesterday's disaster.

"You attacked him for being out with you in the first place," she said. "You acted like he expected something out of you, that he thought you were easy or something and that he planned to take advantage of that. You pretty much called him a little Adventist boy trying to act like he was really worldly."

Actually, these were my exact opinions of him, but all of that should have stayed in my head rather than rush out of my mouth.

"I was just drunk," I said defensively.

She replied, "We were all drinking, Debbie. It was your tone. You were practically spitting in his face. I don't know why you were so mad at him. He really hadn't done anything."

There wasn't much I could say. Gabe represented Gary to me. His girlfriend was a nice girl, too straight for my taste, but I had nothing against her except that she represented the kind of girl these kind of guys ended up marrying.

And I was not.

I was moving away from almost everyone at PUC, feeling more and more as though I didn't belong. I blared Steppenwolf from my dorm room and took up pot and shoplifting. I was flunking out of school and felt happiest at the bars in North Beach in San Francisco, talking to strange men who claimed to be necrophiliacs or watching *Midnight Cowboy* in some dim and dingy theater on Market Street or eating Napoleons and sipping coffee in Sausalito or getting stoned and sneaking into a Lee Michaels concert at the Fillmore West or Winterland Ballroom. My favorite pastimes were sins to

Seventh-day Adventists. I needed these constant distractions. I couldn't be left alone with my feelings of anxiety and loss, crying all the time.

One Saturday, I was trying to corral my friends to go to a rock concert that night in San Francisco. I was willing to drive them in my '69 copper Mustang. At first everyone was for it, but suddenly, people started dropping off. I was furious and knew who was behind ruining my party. It was Mrs. Pluhvoy.

Mrs. Jessie Pluhvoy, dean of women at the college, was determined to keep me on track. She was the one who knew me from when I was in high school at Rio Lindo Academy in Healdsburg. She was trying to stop the trip to San Francisco, mostly because the Fillmore and rock stars were off-limits in a Christian school.

I stormed into her office ready for a fight for chasing away my friends. She agreed she had done just that, calling in each of my compatriots, threatening to call their parents and possibly expel them if they left for San Francisco. This was not the first time she had gotten word of our misdeeds. She'd also heard of a poker game at Bodega Bay.

Mrs. Pluhvoy looked me in the eyes. "I know I can't stop you, Debbie, but I can stop them, and without them, I'm hoping you won't go."

I sat silent and fuming, understanding it was time for me to return to Southern California. I drank too much, snuck off to San Francisco with my friends, and stripped off my clothes in our Gardens of Eden. I missed my mother, never said a word about her trial or her imprisonment, never read her letters to anyone. Depressed and unhappy, I sought escape, anything not to cry and ache. I had no idea where my life was going. I wanted my mom. I wanted her to save me. I had lost Gary, and I seemed too out of control even for my best friends. With all that and my bad grades, I didn't see the point of staying there anymore.

CHAPTER 27:

Return to Southern California

I left PUC at Christmas break during my junior year. I was through. I packed up my Mustang as tightly as I could and pulled out of there, never to return. My friend Genene, who lived in Southern California, decided to drive with me.

We left at night. First, we stopped off at our favorite bar in St. Helena for a few gin gimlets, my drink of choice. We said our goodbyes and popped a couple of black beauties to sober us up for the road. We drove all night and arrived in Los Angeles early the next morning, exhausted and strung out.

I returned to campus a few weeks later to pick up the rest of my stuff. I wasn't sure what was ahead of me, but I knew things weren't good. Too much drinking and pill popping. Too many papers turned in that weren't my own. Too many tests taken that a TA had given me copies of early. By the age of twenty-one, I felt washed up. The only thing that mattered was that my mother was soon to get out of prison.

After five years living in Northern California and spending a lot of time in San Francisco and Sausalito, I had acquired the local snobbery about Southern California. When Genene and I arrived in West Los Angeles, we knocked on the door of one of Sandy's former roommates with whom I had become friends. It was early morning, already sunny and hot. We woke Darlene up. She was surprised when she answered the door. I hadn't even bothered to ask her if we could crash at her house.

I moved in with Darlene after that and promptly lost touch with Genene. With Darlene's permission, I had her couch reupholstered in hot-pink velvet just like my mother's chairs I'd grown up with. I found a job as a receptionist at a law office in Beverly Hills and became friends with the office manager, a pretty redhead named Liz who wore plunging necklines. One day, her pink voile blouse was open so far, I could see her breasts. I thought she didn't know and pointed this out to her. I'll never forget her impish grin and coy response: "It's meant to be that way."

Liz's reply totally made sense to me. From that moment on, I wore plunging necklines, push-up bras, and open blouses that drew attention to my cleavage.

The job didn't last. Most of the attorneys were jerks, arrogant and dismissive. I quit and found another job dispersing reagent bottles to chemistry postdocs at UCLA. I loved this job and enjoyed flirting with the weird postdocs.

In the fall of 1971, I enrolled at Cal State Los Angeles as a sociology major. I loved the reading and my professors, but I continued my habit of cheating.

Darlene had graduated two years earlier, and I ended up in one of her former classes with the same teacher. One of our essay assignments was the same as Darlene's, for which she had earned a C. I used hers exactly as it was and earned an A. That taught me about the subjectivity of grading. I also was best friends with a TA in the sociology department who gave me tests. I studied hard but knew exactly what to study and aced all the exams, bringing my grades up to a respectable GPA.

I was dissuaded from pursuing sociology, though, because of statistics. I managed to pull out a B even though I was flunking because the professor offered a weekend study session, for which I rolled out of bed early that Sunday. He gave anyone who showed up for that session, which was almost nobody, an automatic B. Boy, was I glad I'd attended the study session.

I thought I wanted to be a social worker, but not when I found out how many more statistics classes awaited me. So in 1973, I gave up and quit school again.

CHAPTER 28:

Parents and Children

While I was unsuccessfully searching for what to do with my life, my mother had become the secretary to the head psychiatrist at Frontera: Dr. Dreiser, a distant relative of famed author Theodore Dreiser, who loved my mother and who thought she was different from the rest of the inmates. My mother liked working for her because it earned her a lot of freedom. Dr. Dreiser treated her with respect and dignity, and my mother confided in her, pouring out the truth of her childhood, her loveless marriage, and maybe even some of her prison antics.

The year before my mother was released, the prison opened its doors to the children of the inmates for a Christmas party. The dorms, called houses, were discrete buildings. Each house was throwing its own party. Mom had worked for days decorating her room, such as she had been allowed, for the holiday festivities. My brothers and I were excited about this event.

Guy, Ron, and I were led with the other inmates' children to our mother's house and guided down a narrow hall to the sitting room, which was decorated for Christmas, garland fastened around the guard's station, handmade ornaments dangling from the Christmas tree, and decorations like snowflakes and Santa posters pasted on the walls. Many of the women in prison were good but untrained artists. They did the best they could with what they had, producing crude and unpolished drawings or cutouts. Prison art has the same look as prison tattoos, easily recognizable, the style raw and unrefined, heavy-handed, mostly done in black ink but with perspective and beautiful detail.

The effect of all this, especially the art, was both wonderful and depressing. Christmas didn't quite come alive in the wing of a prison ward. Mom met us in this room and was able to take us down to her cell. It was neat and tidy and small. She had tried to make it cozy, using what she could and what was allowed—a couple of square pillows crocheted by another inmate on her twin bed, which was pressed up against a brick wall painted a dull gray rather than plain red bricks that would have added warmth and color. Arts and crafts picture frames, boxes, beadwork, and drawings were what Mom had used to try to make her cell homey. After my brothers and I closely examined, admired, and complimented Mom's decorating, we didn't know what to do next.

Soon, other inmates, friends of Mom from her hall, stopped by to meet us.

One of the qualities I always liked about my mom was that she adopted people, whom my brothers and I called her orphans. Sandy had been an orphan, and there had been others before Sandy who had moved in with us for a time. Mom's orphans were people whose families either were dead or lived a long way off or were abusive or poor.

Even in prison, Mom had managed to adopt an orphan here and there, someone whose circumstances she believed were worse than hers. She introduced us to one that day. I'll call her Jane.

Mom left us alone in her cell briefly to retrieve Jane and make her come and join us, saying as she went, "She's had a terrible life."

This was how all the stories of Mom's orphans began. Each inmate's history was similar: a violent and abusive father, one or more males who had sexually abused them, alcoholism, extreme neglect. The list of cruelties they had endured was long, and a clear explanation for how they had ended up in prison. Jane's story was no different.

I remember how surprised I was when I saw her. Blond and pale, she was in her early twenties; a junkie who looked more like a preppie, with her bobbed hair, smooth, fine features, and baby face. She had tried suicide more than once.

"I just love your mother," she told me.

My mother loved her orphans the way no one had ever loved them before. She folded them under her wings. I can't remember a holiday that didn't include at least one person who had no place to go and found themselves invited to our family gathering. This is a quality of my mother's that I would later embrace in my own life, listening and watching for someone who needs a place to go on Thanksgiving or Christmas.

After years of allowing only once-a-week visits, Frontera started to let the children of inmates come and spend a weekend in little cottages on the prison grounds. If an inmate was soon to be released and had no marks against her, her children could stay overnight. My mom was a year away from being eligible for parole and had maintained a good record, meaning she was never busted for her shenanigans to supply fellow inmates with everything from makeup to alcohol. I was in my late teens and so excited to have Mom to myself for a weekend. The cottage was clean with a little living room, kitchen, and bedroom with twin beds.

The first night I spent with Mom in one of the cottages, she told me she wanted me to know some things. Her father had died, and that freed her to talk about how abusive he had been. He would strip her naked and whip her with a strap as she crouched at his feet, begging him to stop. Every infraction deserved a whipping, and every whipping began with stripping her naked. "This same bastard, who had me clutching his ankles and begging him to stop, was the one who took me sleighing and ice-skating and bought me hot chocolate."

The beatings stopped when she was sixteen. She'd broken her curfew, and both her parents were waiting up for her. Her father was beside himself with fury. Her mother sat quietly in a chair. My grandfather told my mother to get the strap and he would settle with her upstairs. Instead, she headed straight for the fireplace mantel, picked up a porcelain figurine, raised it above her head, and said, "You're not going to touch me anymore. If you take one more step toward me, I'm going to bash your head in."

Silence. My grandfather turned and walked out of the room.

My mother looked to her mother, sitting pale and speechless, who then slowly lifted herself up by the arms of the chair. She stared back at my mother and said, "You've done nothing but ruin my marriage since the day you were born." And left the room.

"Didn't you hate her?" I asked.

"Hate her?" My mother was incredulous. "What was she supposed to do?"

But I wasn't finished. "Where was Grandma Tubby during those beatings?" I pushed.

"She was at work," my mom said. "She worked all the time. She didn't come home until late at night."

Not satisfied, I pressed further. "Weren't there marks all over you, on your legs?"

"Yes." There was an edge to her voice. She knew where I was going.

"Didn't Tubby see the marks?"

"Yes, I'm sure she did." I could tell my mother could barely speak now.

I was sick to my stomach. I hated Grandpa, but I hated Grandma Tubby even more. "But Mom." I could barely get it out. "She never protected you from him."

My mother's eyes welled with tears. Shaking her head "no," she whispered, "I can't think about that. I just can't think about that."

We never spoke of the abuse again.

I also learned that just before the discovery of my grandfather's illness, my mother was almost removed from the home. Someone had reported the screams. On more than one occasion, he'd locked her in the dark basement, and he once slammed her head into the oven door.

My grandmother Tubby had horror of her own in her childhood. She was the third of four children and always said that only her youngest brother, Joe, loved her. Like my youngest brother, Ron, Joe was the family favorite, an easygoing little boy, able to negotiate the tricky terrain of loving his sister with all his heart without losing favor with his mother. But Joe died young, burned to death in the living room by the fireplace. No one knows how he caught fire. He was wearing his pajamas. My grandmother heard him screaming. She threw her covers off and raced down the stairs toward the hysterical cries for help. By the time she reached him, Joe was engulfed in flames, rolling on the ground. He couldn't be saved. His burns were too severe.

The family's grief was unbearable, and my grandmother's grief never left her. Her mother, already cold and detached with her only daughter, grew even more distant, as though this tragedy were my grandmother's fault. My great-grandmother simply couldn't bear that baby Joe, her favorite, was gone while her daughter still lived. Tubby loved music, but her mother wouldn't pay for lessons, forcing Tubby to sell magazines to pay for them.

My mother resembled my great-grandmother—deep-set blue eyes, thin lips, a pretty woman with potential for meanness in her eyes, flashing anger without warning. Both made clear to their daughters their preference for raising boys.

Yet my mother loved Tubby more than anyone else in the world. While I was growing up, my mother regularly phoned Tubby, who then lived in Portland, Oregon. Once a year, we flew there to stay with her parents.

When we visited my grandparents, Mom and Tubby joked and laughed and shopped and adored each other. I was jealous of my mother's relationship with my grandmother, just as I was jealous of her relationship with Sandy.

There always was tension between my mother and her father, but I hadn't understood the root of it at the time. I didn't know yet about my grandfather's abuse. I just thought he was irritable and cranky. Having his three grandchildren in his house made him worse. More than once, she screamed at her father that if he touched her children, she was leaving with us. I should have taken that as a clue of something, but I wasn't old enough or sophisticated enough to understand. I did know that sometimes my mom fought with her parents about money—because she always needed it, always wanted more.

Tubby was adored and cherished by my mother, but the affection between them was complicated. When Tubby got the phone call that Mom had been arrested for murdering my father, her first response was, "Did she do it?"

CHAPTER 29:

Living with Mom

My life had become a series of periods of waiting.

I waited for Mom's trial. I waited for it to end in acquittal. I waited for her to move to prison so I could visit her there. Then I waited to visit her each week. I waited for her appeals, hoping that one would overturn her conviction. Finally, I waited for her release, which finally happened in 1972. I was twenty-two.

I was in my early twenties, and I didn't have a plan for my own life, no goals except to live with Mom forever. I was stuck in an emotional adolescence.

After she was released from prison, I moved all over Los Angeles County with her, trying to satisfy my need for something she was incapable of giving me. I believed she had a lot to make up to me, which she tried to do in her way. Just like my childhood, I had every material thing I could imagine. I took it all without shame or questions.

Just before my mother was released from prison and after my grandfather had died, my grandmother Tubby sold her home in Loma Linda, bought a green Pinto for Mom, and moved to a house in Panorama City, a planned community tucked between the 405 and the 5 freeways in the northeastern part of the San Fernando Valley, where she, Kimi, and Mom could live together. Leafy tropical plants lined the stone steps to Tubby's house. Everything inside and outside was painted white.

Guy, Ron, and I packed our bags and moved in. Everybody needed to live with Mom. But with all of us there, piles of clothing soon cluttered both the bedrooms and living room. I grew weary of the chaos and returned to my West Los Angeles apartment.

Mom soon felt stifled, too. Tensions developed. From Tubby's point of view, mortgaging her house to help pay for Mom's trial, raising her daughter's baby, moving to California, and buying Mom a car should have assured her of her daughter's devotion. But after seven years in prison, Mom felt she had the right to create a new life.

It was when my mom met David, a retired television writer of westerns like *Bonanza* and *Have Gun—Will Travel*, that Tubby's possessiveness began to stifle my mom. She informed Tubby she planned to move out and raise Kimi on her own. My grandmother responded that if she tried to take Kimi away from her, she would take Mom to court for custody. My mom was stunned and heartbroken. With no money to fight for her daughter, she closed her heart, moved out, and moved on.

I could understand how my grandmother felt after all she had sacrificed for her daughter, and she had raised Kimi as her own since infancy. But, on the other hand, she never protected my mother from the severe abuse of her father. I was angry she had threatened a lawsuit rather than let my mother have Kimi.

I'm sure my vision of my mother raising Kimi was a romantic one, stemming from my desire for things to go back to how they'd once been. Maybe it would have turned out as toxic for Kimi as it had for her brothers and sister, but I like to believe that my mother would have been a better person if she'd been able to raise her beloved baby girl. Losing Kimi further hardened her. We saw Kimi periodically during these years, but it was not enough for me to feel like she was my sister, not enough to see how alone she was when my grandmother died, not enough to recognize when she needed help. Ron and his wife, Cyndy, were there for her, but I wasn't until it was too late.

Someone gave Mom the money to begin her new life. She left Lucille Miller behind her and changed her name to Reni Maxwell. In 1972, Mom found a nice apartment in North Hollywood on Moorpark, and I moved in with her. My bedroom window framed a tree-lined street that was hushed and peaceful, as far from the allure of West Hollywood as one can get.

To many, Hollywood is synonymous with glamour, fame, scandalous love affairs, and nasty divorces. But North Hollywood, in the San Fernando Valley, is not distinguished by any of that. We had almost no furniture except for my hot-pink velvet couch and a pair of small smoked-glass coffee tables. We didn't even have a television or stereo, which was fine with both of us. Gary, my old boyfriend from college who had broken my heart, came to visit me in this apartment. He spent the night, but I felt too much anxiety to make love. It had been too long. He had broken my heart, and now it seemed he wanted to act as if nothing had transpired between us.

The next morning, he brought me coffee and toast, using one of the smoked-glass coffee tables as a tray. I could not warm up to him. I wanted him to leave, and eventually, he got the hint. But the minute he was gone, I wanted him to come back. I wanted to make love. I wanted all the things I'd been unable to ask for just moments earlier. I couldn't take the chance he might hurt me again. He didn't apologize for the past. I was angry that he pretended nothing unusual was happening. I wanted to marry him. Instead, I let him walk out.

As for Mom, I didn't know or much care what she was up to as long as I could live with her. My expectation was that she would take care of me and choose me as her best friend. I didn't even offer to pay rent.

All that changed in a hurry. Mom had always taken matters into her own hands: signing loan documents without my father's knowledge for the Bella Vista house, sleeping with other men to satisfy her libido. She was a survivor, and prison had only enhanced her skills. Now, without money or a job, she turned to what she knew best: schemes and deceptions that eventually brought her down.

I wasn't ready for any of it. When I was young, I couldn't do anything about what she said or did. Now I was an adult. I felt guilty over her time in prison, that I was free and she was not. But in some strange way, I felt that she needed to make it up to me. I was confused and stuck and needy. I couldn't move on. But for all the anxiety her methods caused me, I knew that *she* could. So I stayed.

One morning while I was sipping my coffee, my feet up on the couch, my mom's bedroom door opened and out came a tall, chubby Black man—I'll call him Jack—wearing pink rubber rollers in his hair. He looked shocked to see me, and I must have looked at him equally shocked, because my mother had never mentioned having a lover, except for David. I wondered if he was still in the picture.

Neither of us spoke. He made coffee and carried two mugs back to the bedroom and shut the door.

I sat there, furious. What the hell! Prison had followed her, pairing her with this guy. I knew one of Mom's inmates had set up this connection for her. *She's madly in love with David, so what is going on?* I asked myself. She clearly was sleeping with this guy. At the time, I just shoved my questions out of my head. I did not want to know. Yet soon the answer became apparent.

As always, I was afraid to say anything, afraid she would banish me just like she'd banished me to my bedroom growing up because the sight of me enraged her.

Eventually, Mom explained her relationship with Jack. He was her partner in a fencing scheme. Jack was the fence. Mom was the thief. She bore the higher risk. Mom learned how to steal high-end quality goods, clothing, purses, and other luxury items. She sold them to Jack, who resold them for a profit.

Mom had left prison knowing how to garden and how to file, not much help in the world before her. One of the inmates gave her the phone number of the man who could help her make some money fast. As soon as she got out, Jack had been waiting for her call. Mom was sleeping with Jack because she had to.

CHAPTER 30:

Al

In less than six months, we moved to another apartment in North Hollywood. The living room divided the two bedrooms and baths. A black vinyl couch with wooden arms sat on the green shag carpet and took up too much space in the living room. A fake Tiffany lamp hung above the dining room table. The pink couch and coffee tables disappeared. I never asked Mom about that.

One morning, Mom rushed into my room, frantic because Jack was there and David, her television writer boyfriend, had called and was on his way.

Just as when she was in prison and I had smuggled in contraband to provide her illicit income, she had turned to me for help. My instructions were to claim Jack was my friend if David showed up.

Reluctantly, I complied.

We celebrated our first Christmas together that December. It was clear Mom had done some shopping—well, shoplifting. The gift she was excited to give me was a red velvet Little Red Riding Hood cape. When I opened the box, I was so disappointed. Nobody wore red velvet capes. She had always had such good taste. I didn't want to hurt her feelings. I realized Mom was showing me love the only way she could, by giving me stuff.

I pretended I loved it, but I couldn't fool her. Just like the couch and tables, the cape mysteriously disappeared. Again, I didn't ask any questions.

Mom always was on the lookout for a catch for me. Her criterion was a prospect's money-earning potential. In that way, she was much like millions of other moms. But she took finding a masculine paycheck to a fine art.

One Saturday night, I was hanging out by the pool, sipping Tanqueray gin and tonics with Mom, my brothers, and their friend Sonny—a stocky, good-looking guy, a player, whom I was flirting with—when a handsome, Italian, Burt Reynolds look-alike walked up and introduced himself as Al.

Al had perfectly coiffed black hair and eyelashes that would make any woman jealous. Ignoring Sonny, I turned to Al and learned he was in law school and lived two doors down from Mom and me. I was nervous and self-conscious, because I immediately felt attracted to him. He was smooth and charming.

Al left soon after he met us. Once he did, I turned my attention back to Sonny, who spent the night with me.

A few days later, Al invited me to a car show featuring the latest models at the Coliseum in downtown Los Angeles.

According to Mom, Al was a catch: He was good-looking, was in law school, and drove an orange 240Z Datsun. She immediately loved Al and tried to guide me down the path of manipulation to snag him, which didn't feel right to me.

She took the first step for the trap after Al invited me to the car show. She picked out what I should wear—white pants with a low-cut red top, all stolen. I also glued on false eyelashes my mother bought for me. This was my first and last time wearing them. To Mom, looking fabulous was the most important part of my first date with Al. She liked me best when she dressed me up. I was Mom's mannequin.

I loved cars, loved wandering around looking at my favorite cars, including the Ford Mustang's newest generation, a bright-orange hatchback polished to a sheen. Gliding through the slick new models, my new eyelashes began to feel thick and heavy. I kept rubbing my right eye until it began to burn. Al checked for a stray eyelash but instead saw thin red lines, which turned out to be broken blood vessels. I was embarrassed. My eye got so painful, we had to leave. It turned out I had a corneal abrasion from the eyelashes scraping my eye. The only cure was to not touch the eye until the redness disappeared.

We drove back to the valley to an optometrist friend of Al's for the diagnosis. I was certain Al wouldn't want to see me again.

I was not yet a cook, but for Mom, that wasn't a problem. She convinced me to invite Al to dinner—and to my surprise, he accepted. She brought home everything I needed: a frozen Stouffer's spinach soufflé and greens for a salad and sliced tomatoes on the side. Mom set the table and gently coaxed the cooked soufflé out of the tin pan onto two plates. Al arrived for dinner and proceeded to gush over the soufflé, which I couldn't understand.

Later, when I told Mom how much Al liked the soufflé, she responded, "That's perfect; it means he thinks you made it."

This did not sit well with me either. I felt embarrassed, like I'd tricked him. I'd assumed he would know the spinach soufflé was frozen; it wasn't that good.

I was learning how to catch a man. It was working so far.

A few years later, Al told me Mom tucked a check into his shirt pocket. "Take Deb to dinner," she instructed. She did this a few times, and every time, the checks bounced.

Al and I had great sex, but we didn't get along that well. Al was macho and controlling, and I had a mind of my own. But he was the guy my mom picked for me, so I wanted him.

When I first met Al, I was still in love with Gary and my broken heart was guarded. Al was the direction of security and status, perhaps a pathway to a family, which was something I'd always wanted, or perhaps longed for.

CHAPTER 31:

Pulling Away

During the time we lived in North Hollywood, despite my need for my mother, I struggled for a more balanced relationship with her. I decided that I could not be kept waiting for her like I had had to do after school.

One night, she and I had plans to meet for dinner in Toluca Lake at Patys, a popular restaurant that was a cross between a café and a diner. I arrived first. She was late. I waited fifteen minutes, and when Mom hadn't arrived, I drove home.

When she got home, she nicely asked me if she had the wrong time because I hadn't been at the restaurant when she arrived.

I turned to her, looked her in the eye, and said, "Mom, I will never wait for you again."

She was never late again.

One day, about a year after Mom's release from prison, I heard the phone ringing inside our apartment just as I was getting home from work. I struggled with the key, finally unlocked the door, and rushed to the phone. It was a male voice: "This is sergeant so-and-so from the North Hollywood Police Department, and I'm looking for a Reni Maxwell."

I froze. "She isn't here," I replied defensively.

"Do you know where she is, when she'll be back?" he asked.

"No," I replied.

"Maybe you're the one I'm looking for?" he asked.

Suddenly my fear turned to hatred. "No, I'm not!" I snapped and hung up.

Mom didn't come home. I was a wreck. Several hours later, one of her attorneys called. She had been arrested for shoplifting a T-shirt from I. Magnin, a high-end department store. After all the expensive clothing she had purloined, she got caught stealing a T-shirt. An expensive one, yes, but a T-shirt. The police had taken her to Sybil Brand, a women's jail atop a hill in Los Angeles County, mostly for women awaiting trial or moving to prison.

I should have been furious. Instead, I felt my world crashing again. I sobbed. I was terrified of what would happen to me. I'd left myself solely in her hands, and I was nowhere and no one without her. I never asked how she spent her time. We lived well, both our closets filled with expensive clothes: slacks, summer tops, and my favorite long nightgowns by Emilio Pucci, an Italian designer known for his psychedelic kaleidoscope sleepwear, with swirls of complementary lavenders, pinks, and blues, silky to touch. I had never asked where the clothes came from, even though I knew.

I went to visit her at the jail. We sat on a cement block, and she said, "I knew when I was arrested this time that I was guilty, that I probably would be sent back to prison."

Exactly my fear.

She told me she had been sitting in her cell by an opened barred window when a slight breeze and peacefulness washed over her. "I started praying to God that if he would keep me from going back to prison, I would never do anything illegal again. I rocked back and forth, crying, begging God to forgive me when a huge tumbleweed floated out from my chest, rolled through the bars, out the window. I knew those were my sins," she explained. "I knew God was giving me another chance. I was going to be okay."

She was released from Sybil Brand the next morning and came home. She didn't keep her promise to God. I don't think she even believed in him, so not keeping her end of the bargain didn't rankle her at all.

A friend of mine at work had a cat who had given birth to four kittens. Two had found homes. The last two needed adopting. I wanted one of them. My mom was open to almost any kind of pet. When she was a girl, she had begged her parents to buy her a dog. They'd refused. When I talked about adopting a kitten, she was excited. She chose the quiet little tabby over the marmalade who was climbing the curtains.

That little baby mewed all the way home. By the time we got home, Mom had named her Tres Jolie, meaning "very pretty."

Mom tried to make Jolie hers, but the kitten made another choice. We discovered this when Jolie fell from our balcony and was hiding under a car. Mom tried her best to coax her out, but the kitten was having none of it. Finally, Mom ran up the stairs to our apartment

"She wants you. You have to go down and get her."

Wearing my pink chenille bathrobe, I crouched down on my hands and knees on the pavement, peeked under the car, and saw Jolie sitting on her haunches, facing me. I called her name, and that little baby marched right to me. I picked her up, grease and all, cradled her in my arms, and carried her back upstairs. I was in love. Here was someone who wanted my whole attention, my love, and I had so much to give. I was so happy she'd chosen me.

Several months after her shoplifting arrest, Mom decided she wanted to live alone. She moved to a single in the Toluca Hills Oakwood Apartments off Barham Boulevard in Toluca Lake, a small, cozy town nestled next to a natural lake between an exclusive golf club and pricey homes around the lake's shores.

I stayed in our building and moved into a single, open-space apartment cleverly sectioned into a kitchen, living room, and bedroom. A counter separated the kitchen and living room. You had to step up into the bedroom, which had a wrought-iron divider about three feet tall to create a partition from the living room. A basket chair hung from the ceiling in the living room.

Al worked for UPS in the mornings, studied in the afternoons, and attended law school in the evenings. My life curled itself around his. I attended all of his baseball games, even though I didn't like baseball. His friends became my friends. While he studied, I spent many hours folded up on my red paisley bedspread reading thrillers like Sidney Sheldon's *The Other Side of Midnight*, about a young girl's terror because she is being menaced and doesn't know by whom or why. Jolie snuggled beside me. I learned to cook in this apartment.

I was twenty-three years old, and I felt like I was building a life.

CHAPTER 32:

Unraveling

Soon enough, my relationship with Al began to unravel, weakened by extreme ups and downs. One night, I slapped him and tried to take that back in a hurry. Another time, we were in his apartment fighting and he threw me on his waterbed; my back barely missed the wooden frame. But then he'd do something to make it up to me, like buying me a necklace with a gold heart and the inscription "To Debra Love Al 12-25-1973." I didn't know enough to recognize how messed up this was.

One night, I was out with him at his friend's house. Their poker game continued late into the night. I lay curled up on a couch and asked Al several times if we could go home. He responded with that same angry look my mom often gave me. I finally threw the car keys at him, which infuriated and embarrassed him in front of his poker pals. He refused to leave.

We became perpetually angry at each other. During a luau my mother threw at her apartment complex's recreation room, Al left the room, I assumed to go to the men's room. He did not come back. I panicked and started to cry. My mom assured me he must have gone home.

He stayed away for three days.

We remained off and on for a long time after that. At one point, we moved in together for a while. Mom had recently moved again and was living in a single in the Mediterranean Village in West Hollywood.

Al and I spent Christmas Eve with her that year. If he was ever going to propose to me, this was the time. He gave me a beautiful blouse and a couple of other gifts, but he never handed me a ring box.

My disappointment was palpable. I was crushed, and both Mom and Al knew why.

It was over, and yet not yet over because I didn't leave him.

Delia, a friend from work, knew I liked uppers. She and her husband, an Estonian named Taro, invited me to dinner, a surprise because I didn't think she liked me. He was a tall, blond postdoc in one of the sciences at UCLA. Delia was brunette, fair, and considerably shorter than Taro. They had met when she was a UCLA undergraduate. Delia didn't tell me anything except that she was eager to use her new Wedgwood china and have an excuse to show off her new culinary talents by serving crème spinach crepes. I arrived to the spotless little apartment of these blissful newlyweds. The table was already set. I was living with Al at the time, but I came alone. We enjoyed a glass of wine and gossiped about work before dinner. Her crepes were creamy, with a touch of nutmeg flavor—delicious.

To me, theirs seemed like a let's-play-house kind of marriage—with her cooking new dishes for her husband, adoring everything he did. Plus, they had lots of good sex that she was very vocal about, sharing details whenever anyone at work would listen.

After dinner, out came one of Delia's new silver trays with little colored glasses in the shape of tiny wine glasses and two bottles of liqueur, one chocolate and one apricot. While we sipped liqueurs and smoked cigarettes, she revealed the star of the evening.

I, of course, was no stranger to drugs. I had been popping cross tops and black beauties for years.

"I invited you to dinner for a special reason," Delia announced. "Taro and I tried a new drug this weekend that I know you'll love because you're into uppers, and this is the Cadillac of uppers."

I was excited and honored.

As much as I liked certain drugs, I was not one to easily try *new* drugs. I always had steered clear of psychedelics. I'd heard the urban legend about a guy who landed in the emergency room because too many tabs of LSD had convinced him he was an orange. He became fixated on his navel. The only doctor who could touch him without him screaming was the one who convinced him he wouldn't peel him. Urban legend or not, I was convinced this would happen to me.

Neither was I into downers. My brothers had gone through that phase in high school, popping "reds," which I believe was the street name for Seconal. One time, I went to the movies with my brothers and watched them stumble into the theater and plop into their seats, only to slide to the floor or nod off and snore. This was no fun for me, particularly because it became my responsibility to keep pulling them up off the floor and propping them back into their seats.

What I did like was the illusion speed gave me of being busy and getting lots done. The fact that Delia called this new white powder "the Cadillac of uppers" was the only reason I was willing to give it a try.

I instinctively took to the ritual of tapping a little mound of white powder onto the coffee table, chopping it carefully with a razor blade, front to back, back to front, scraping and chopping until it felt smooth beneath the blade. Dividing the pile into six lines, cut in, scrap aside, one sweep of the blade to make a line, tidy it up, cut into the pile again, repeat. I loved it. Putting a rolled-up hundred-dollar bill to my nose and vacuuming up a thin white line felt perfectly natural, even on the first try. The subtle numbing of the back of my nostrils, the slightly acrid taste of the cocaine sliding down my throat, felt pleasant, even soothing. I couldn't stop snorting the stuff until it was gone. I felt euphoric. The second a little anxiety surfaced, I wanted more.

Delia and Taro were thrilled to see how well I had taken to it. Delia warned me that it might be difficult to go to sleep and that I should take a Valium. Knowing it would keep me up made me anxious, but knowing there was a remedy for this immediately made me feel better.

When I left my friend's apartment, I hallucinated that an eagle on the freeway was swooping past the driver's side of my windshield. I believed it was real. I clutched the steering wheel tightly, leaning forward, shoulders hunched, steering carefully to avoid hitting the bird. I was on the 405 Freeway, driving north over the Sepulveda Pass, not the best place to be imagining things. I wasn't frightened, though. I just didn't want that huge bird's guts and feathers smashed against my windshield. That eagle obstructed much of my view until I got off the freeway.

This experience taught me nothing. When I arrived home, I crept into my apartment. Al was asleep. I took a Valium and joined him.

Seeing my puffy eyes in the mirror the next morning did not dissuade me from snorting cocaine again. I did not acknowledge cocaine as a serious drug. It wasn't considered addictive, and I didn't even know it could cause hallucinations.

In 1977, while I was living with Al, I enrolled in college for the third time at Cal State University Northridge, taking night classes to finish my BA in sociology. I quit again after one year. Life with Al had become boring. We barely had sex after we moved into that apartment. Al tried harder than I did to make it work, except for one scary night.

Mom had invited us to dinner. She now lived in a two-bedroom, two-bath apartment in the Mediterranean Village. Mom and I must have had a conversation about my moving back in with her. Al and I fought on the way to her apartment. Never one to smooth things over, I sassed him as we walked toward the door of the apartment, which sent him into a rage. I knocked on Mom's door, and before she answered, Al grabbed my neck with both hands and began choking me, his palms closing in tighter and tighter. I couldn't breathe and realized that if my mom didn't open the door soon, I was in danger. Just then, the knob turned, and Al let go.

I never said anything to my mom. I believed I deserved it. Al and I never talked about it.

But my problems with Al led to more chaos.

A small group of us became friends, including hip and street-savvy Jimmy. He had his own home in the woods in nearby Sunland. He always had cocaine. He laughed, made me laugh, and teased me. I loved the energy. I was trying to graduate from college, living with my boyfriend, cheating on my boyfriend with Jimmy, doing drugs all the time.

Things eventually cooled off with Jimmy, but I ended up leaving Al anyway, finally. He didn't make any effort to make me stay. I didn't care.

I was ill-equipped to take on the world. Part of that was my longing for a real mother, but another factor was the fundamentalist religion to which I had been born. My life had been structured within the expectations of that religion. I would enter an Adventist college to find a husband. He would be a doctor or a dentist who had graduated from Loma Linda University. We would have children and raise them the same way my husband and I had been raised.

I did not know anything about life outside of Adventism. I had been raised to be frightened of the world beyond my religion. We had to stay with our own kind or the devil might destroy us. I didn't question this. I believed what I'd been taught and had no desire to live any differently from the way I had been brought up. I wasn't prepared to do anything else.

Gary had met all those qualifications. He was the kind of man I'd been raised to marry, an Adventist doctor. I was already a long way from Adventism when I met Gary, but still, I'd loved him with all my heart.

Al was nothing like Gary, except that he seemed to know as well as Gary had about the truth of our future together before I did.

CHAPTER 33:

Old Patterns

In 1978, Al finally broke up with me for good. I moved back with Mom into another two-bedroom, two-bath apartment in the Mediterranean Village on Larrabee, set between Sunset and Santa Monica Boulevard. Apartments surrounded an oval pool. Lounge chairs framed it. Ferns and palms created a tropical atmosphere. A koi fishpond bubbled along one of the walkways leading to other apartments. The lobby's red terra-cotta tiles along with cushioned wicker sofas and chairs created a soft elegance. Other wicker sets tucked themselves into outdoor patios set back among the lush greenery.

It was in this lovely Mediterranean setting where I became the center of Mom's universe—her best friend, her adored daughter. During these years, I had the best relationship with my mom I was ever going to have. Yet I was deeply depressed.

I was working a nowhere job at UCLA and had dropped out of college three times without earning my degree. I lacked dreams or ambitions except for living with Mom and trying not to think about what a waste my life had been so far. I was good looking. Men were attracted to me.

As long as I didn't have to be quiet with myself, I could pretend life was a blast.

Drugs and alcohol masked the truth of my life, but when the sun came up, and I was still rattling around desperate to go to sleep, anxiety washed through me and kept me awake. When I tried to sleep, my anxiety increased. I just tossed and turned, wishing I were dead. I hated myself and would promise myself that if I could just sleep, I would change. When I was high, I had all the confidence in the world, determined to finish college. I'd always been a voracious reader: Hawthorne, Steinbeck, Twain, and the British poet and novelist Thomas Hardy were my favorites. But I could not put my skills to practical use. My future looked unavoidably grim.

As for Mom, she found a job at Lynn Carol employment agency. She loved it, was good at it, and it paid well. She had the perfect skills—she was outgoing, friendly, social, and a scammer. She was so successful that she became a manager. She didn't come at things with ego. If one of her employees was a prima donna but a whiz at connecting with companies and with clients as well as making money, my mother's philosophy was to keep the prima donna happy. Her employees loved her. Though her ambition, along with her desire for fast money, would eventually be her downfall, for now, we were as steady as we'd ever been.

Mom and I were a mother-daughter combo everyone wanted to hang out with. I met a lot of people because of my mom's outgoing personality. People loved her and wanted to be in her company. When you were with her, she gave you her full attention, had you laughing and feeling good about yourself. She told you secrets, which made you feel special. Except for her children, people kept her confidence.

While Mom was always the draw, I benefited from her popularity. I was the daughter of this gregarious, outgoing, beautiful, clever woman with exquisite taste. My status resulted from her status, and she was more than happy to share it with me. I didn't have a separate self. Most of the guys who worked at the nearby Palm Restaurant lived in the Mediterranean Village. Others worked in the movie industry or downtown in the Fashion District. It was a time of baby boomer decadence. I wanted to be with my mom, fit in with the "cool" crowd engaging in perpetual entertainment.

It all revolved around the pool. Mom sunbathed with a glass of white wine, a couple of ice cubes bobbing around the rim. Those days brought back warm memories of when we were whole as a family, spending weekends in Corona del Mar, eating blueberry pancakes soaked with boysenberry syrup, followed by a day at the local beach. My brothers and I were good swimmers who prided ourselves on swimming past the buoys. I am fair-skinned, but I've always tanned easily. My mom and my brothers and I spent each summer a pretty shade of copper.

Mom loved a particular piano lounge in our neighborhood on Sunset Boulevard, dimly lit, a baby grand surrounded by red leather stools for customers listening to Art the piano man caressing the piano keys to romantic melodies such as "Someday My Prince Will Come," seducing lonely women sipping wine as they daydreamed the song was for them and them exclusively. At least, that's what my mother believed. I'd been there only one time before, and a scout from *Penthouse* magazine named Sandy Roads had approached me about doing a shoot for the magazine. I declined, but she left me her card. *Penthouse* was trash to me. Had it been *Playboy*, I would have agreed.

The same evening, a handsome man dressed in a white linen suit and wearing a panama hat stood at the bar and indicated I should join him. I don't remember his name, but I learned he was an Appalachian Mountain boy come to the city. He was leaving the lounge for a nightclub down the street and invited me to go with him. When we stepped onto the boulevard, a white-on-white-interior Cadillac pimpmobile sporting chrome bumpers and three mounted exterior white and chrome hard-shell tire covers was waiting for us at the curb. I found this both hilarious and embarrassing but said nothing. As I stood on the curb, he opened his trunk, revealing a cache of guns neatly lined up.

Someone not raised by my mother would have walked away, but not me. This type of person was familiar to me. I was not afraid. Visiting my mom in prison and living with her had warped me. For seven years, I'd snuck contraband in to my mother, risking my own freedom. I was following in Mom's morally ambiguous footsteps.

As I stood looking at the guns in the trunk, I knew from experience that this guy was the low man on the totem pole of a mob.

I saw him one more time in his boozy, smoke-filled apartment, where the roughness of who he was surfaced. I was sitting on his lap listening to his story when I asked him a question that pricked something inside him. He got very stiff and warned me away. I can't recall the specifics. I do recall my reaction. I left and never saw him again.

He called me one more time. He did not understand what had happened. I was afraid of him now. I couldn't explain that I couldn't allow his world to collide into my world. When I left his apartment that day, my attraction ended.

My two best friends in the Mediterranean Village were Celeste, who was often mistaken for Faye Dunaway because of her blond hair and high cheekbones, and Diana, an adorable, shameless liar and thief. These two women, their boyfriends, and the Palm's waiters introduced me to the West Hollywood scene and nightlife. West Hollywood was—and still is—primarily a gay community, sometimes called Boystown. Flashy bars, expensive restaurants. We frequented The Rainbow Room and Whiskey a Go Go, with its kaleidoscope of lights along Sunset Boulevard. Living there was wild, and I loved it.

Gigi, the Palm's maître d', had once been Celeste's boyfriend, and they were still good friends. We never paid for our drinks or lobster dinners. The boys from the Palm were easygoing, made lots of money in tips, and then lost it playing the horses and sustaining their drug habits. They moved around from the New York Palm to the Hawaii Palm to the Beverly Hills Palm. They were good-looking, well-read, friendly, and hip.

Bobby was sexier than he was handsome, salt and pepper hair and piercing blue eyes. He was the one I developed a crush on. Bobby lived with his girlfriend, but that was beside the point. We were a gang. Celeste and I often strolled on summer evenings to the Palm for a drink. During our sunbathing and swimming at the pool, Bobby and I often hung out together. At some point, it came to light that Bobby had easy access to Quaaludes, and I had easy access to Percodan since I had it prescribed for an intestinal disorder I'd been treating for most of my adult life. While I preferred Quaaludes, Bobby preferred Percodan, so we traded.

One night, Bobby and I sat on my bed doing lines of coke, believing we were involved in a deep philosophical conversation.

We didn't sleep together very many times before I got pregnant.

I didn't tell anyone but Celeste. I knew I had to tell Bobby, even though I didn't want to keep the baby. One Saturday night, Celeste and a group of us walked to the Palm for dinner. Bobby was working, and I intended to tell him.

Coked up, popping a Quaalude along with gin and tonics, gave me the courage to tell him. I slurred in his ear that I was pregnant. He did not react. It was as if he hadn't heard me, and I was too embarrassed to repeat myself. When I got home and crawled into bed, I started to cry, partly because of Bobby's reaction and partly because I couldn't remember how many Quaaludes I'd ingested. Right before I fell asleep, I asked God to please let me wake up in the morning. He did.

I arranged to take care of my pregnancy problem without ever following up with Bobby.

I didn't stop hanging out with Bobby, but it wasn't until after the abortion that I got the courage to ask him why he hadn't responded when I'd told him I was pregnant.

His answer: "I thought you were kidding."

There were other doomed relationships. Dennis Roberts, stocky and overweight, had grown rich designing sunglasses for Elvis Presley and Elton John and owned the Optic Boutique on Sunset Boulevard. He drove a Mercedes and a metallic-brown Rolls-Royce Corniche. Like me, Dennis was a mess. He had a terrible cocaine problem and lived a debauched life. He made it clear he liked me, and I felt flattered that such a rich man found me fun and interesting. I felt comfortable with Dennis, too. Because I was broken, I fell in love with his brokenness.

He began taking me to dinner at Dan Tana's in Beverly Hills, where we both ordered veal chops and hung out with our friends. We checked on his stores. We were easy together. He was soft with me, and I found myself falling in love with him. I can't say we were boyfriend and girlfriend, but we were lovers.

I knew about Dennis's cocaine problem and that he hired prostitutes and held wild parties at his house. Except for using coke with him sometimes, I largely compartmentalized this side of his life and didn't engage in it too much. I didn't care what he did when he wasn't with me. He was good to me.

I spent a lot of time at his house. He had a grand piano in his living room. Standing in the kitchen one night, I heard someone playing the piano, the cocktail lounge tune "Send in the Clowns." I crept to the living room, and there sat Dennis at his piano, swaying in contentment. His piano was in the living room that was not used, so even though I might have glanced at it while passing from one room to another, it didn't occur to me that anyone played it.

His bedroom was always dark. Heavy black curtains covered his regular curtains to block the sunlight after a night of cocaine. One night, we were sitting on his bed sniffing cocaine and drinking gin when Dennis crawled off the bed, stepped into his walk-in closet to pull a box down from a shelf, and returned to the bed. He wanted to show me a stack of compromising photos of women he'd taken. Photo after photo were women posing suggestively with no clothes on; others wore skimpy lingerie, heads thrown back, holding their crotches.

I got into the photos until he asked me if I would pose for him and said that he had the costumes.

"I will never end up in that box, Dennis," I said.

"Can I just take a picture of you naked?" he asked.

I said no again.

He shrugged and put the box back on its shelf, and we never spoke of it again.

No matter what frame of mind I was in, I was not going to be exploited this way. I couldn't imagine being a girl in one of those photos for him to drag down to entice another woman to play his game.

When I sobered up many years later, I became friends in a Cocaine Anonymous meeting with a former madam whom

Dennis had often called to his parties. She once laughed, saying, "You went up there and gave it all away for free. I went up there and got paid for it." But I think one of the things Dennis liked about me was just that—that I just wanted to be with him because I enjoyed spending time with him.

One night when he was dropping me off, I was filled with love. I hesitated before I got out of the car, trying to summon up the courage to tell him I loved him. He put his arm around my shoulder and said, "I know, I know."

I would have married him, taken him warts and all. Thank God he knew better. When I moved away from the Mediterranean Village, I never saw him again. I later heard he died before he turned forty.

When I turned thirty, my mom threw me a whopping birthday party. We invited everyone we knew in the Mediterranean Village. My zodiac sign is the crab, so Mom ordered a beautiful crab-shaped white cake, white frosting outlined with silver dots of candy. Jai, Mom's friend in the building, was a caterer from one of the Caribbean Islands. He created delicious hors d'oeuvres. This was before Dennis and I went our separate ways, so he was also there and brought me a silly gift, wontons with Oscar Wilde aphorisms on them. In the middle of the raucous party, he invited a few of us, including Celeste, to relax in his Jacuzzi. We jumped at this idea and left my party for Dennis's house without a word to my mom.

There were so many people, nobody noticed we had slipped out at first. I later heard that my mom brought out my cake, lit the candles, and called for me. No response. Those of us who'd trekked up to Dennis's house stayed there partying until the sun came up. I don't know how I got home, but I do know that the next day, I was overcome with guilt for ditching my own party when my mom had gone to so much trouble.

Mom was great at parties, but in other ways, she didn't parent me. She never encouraged me to return to college to get my degree. Instead, she taught me to live in the moment, with no thought for consequences. And I absorbed that lesson completely. Perhaps that's why I never felt like the grown-up, probably because I lost my parents when I still needed so badly to be parented.

One summer, Diana asked me if I wanted to fly to Acapulco. My mother and brothers chipped in to help pay for my trip.

Americans flocked to Acapulco for its discos, restaurants, and hotels, and it was known to be a good place to spend a decadent weekend. On our first night there, the handsome disco managers sent us drinks and twirled us around the dance floor to Gloria Gaynor's "I Will Survive." Tanned and wearing a red disco dress, high on alcohol and cocaine, dancing under the winking strobe lights, I gave myself to the music, tears rolling down my cheeks in ecstasy.

We ended up in bed with a couple of the managers that night and woke up in the morning, hungover and in a house on the top of a hill, which we tiptoed out of laughing and lost, circling around until we found our way back to our hotel.

On the last night at the disco we had frequented the most, we soon realized we were no longer the newest girls in town and no longer an attraction for the managers. As our egos deflated, Diana leaned over to tell me that her rich sugar daddy wanted to treat us to a bottle of Dom Pérignon. I suspected she was lying, and when the bill came, I found out I was right. She asked me for $50, claiming she would reimburse me when we got home.

That never happened.

Despite knowing Diana was a liar, I let myself be taken in again when she suggested we trade purses for a few days, her Vuitton bag with my Gucci bag my mother had given me. Soon, Diana wanted to swap back the bags. I handed over her Vuitton, but she told me she had left my bag at work. She never returned my Gucci. And I never confronted her about it. That ended the friendship.

The timing of that coincided with Mom deciding to move to Marina del Rey. Of course, I moved with her.

CHAPTER 34:

Adrift

The new apartment was on Tahiti Way in Marina del Rey, a luxurious place facing one of the inlets from the harbor where expensive boats and yachts docked. My bedroom faced one of the docks, but what I could see wasn't as important as what I could hear: the creaking sound of boats rocking on their moorings, the water lapping against the posts of the dock and the boat's hull, halyards clanging—a chorus singing a song of security as I drifted off to sleep.

Despite the tranquil setting, there were signs that living with Mom wouldn't last. Early on, she ordered a new couch and love seat and instructed me to declaw Jolie. I couldn't believe she'd asked this of me, but my fear of living without my mother overcame me and I acquiesced. The procedure was legal at the time, but I knew it was cruel.

Within days after her declawing, Jolie tumbled off the living room balcony, just as she'd fallen when she was a kitten. When we realized her spill, I cried, knowing how helpless she was without her claws.

Fortunately, she'd fallen directly into the ivy and hunkered down until she heard my voice and meowed.

There were times during this period when I experienced happiness and discovery. Sailing, for example, gave me joy. Celeste had moved back to San Pedro, and she'd grown up sailing to Catalina. Celeste owned a CAL20, so we'd sail over on weekends, scudding around the bay in the whaler. I loved to wash my hair in the ocean and rinse it out with a bucket of fresh water on the boat. We devoured Spam and eggs for breakfast. Everything tastes delicious on a boat. I felt peaceful and free. When Celeste and I were gliding through the water, small waves splashing us, salty air stirring us, I believed I knew how to sail.

One afternoon, Celeste and I were sailing around San Pedro Harbor when the wind began to pick up. Celeste needed to move to the bow to drop the jib, and she gave me the job of keeping the mainsail in the right position to keep the boat from heeling too far over. It sounded easy enough—use the boom keeping the mainsail steady so the boat didn't heel too far one way or the other.

The wind tossed the boat. It was getting much harder to handle the till and work the mainsail at the same time. When it hit me that I was in control, I was horrified. I panicked and couldn't remember the position of the sail I needed to hold. As Celeste weaved her way back to me, the boat heeled so far over, it began taking in water; the only reason Celeste didn't go overboard was that she grabbed the mast as she yelled to me how to get the boat upright again. I don't know how I managed or if I managed, but the boat righted itself. Had Celeste gone overboard, I would not have known how to rescue her.

Celeste introduced me to her friend Brian, who lived on his CAL29 and worked in the boatyard. With his bleach-blond hair and bronze tan, he was every bit the Southern

California ideal. I began driving down to San Pedro each weekend to sail with him. Sometimes I raced with him, though I got seasick any time the spinnaker was lifted.

One evening around eight, Celeste called me to join Brian and her on his boat for a midnight sail to Catalina. What seemed like a million stars twinkled on the water. We sipped hot toddies.

I took for granted that I didn't need an invite to spend weekends with Brian. I believed we were an item. At Christmastime, I gave him a 14K-gold anchor on a gold chain and a gram of coke. He fastened it around his neck until the night he tore it off and threw it at me, announcing he didn't like cocaine. I was embarrassed and hurt. I didn't understand that he didn't think we were an item. I didn't take the hint.

The following weekend, I schlepped back down to Brian's boat. I heard voices as I got closer to the dock where he moored his boat, a female. I thought it was a friend of his. I got just far enough to see into the galley only to find him in bed with another woman. I was humiliated, turned around, and drove sobbing to Celeste's place. When she opened the door, tears were still streaming down my cheeks. She told me she wasn't aware that Brian was seeing anyone else or she would have called me.

I was more devastated than I should have been. On the one hand, I didn't consider myself his girlfriend. I didn't love him. The sex was not fulfilling. I wanted to sail. I wanted to believe I was welcomed at any time on Brian's boat. I had become a sailor, and now it was gone. I no longer had an identity; the tranquility, the breeze, the salty air, and the joy were now hushed, leaving a hole where a sailboat had once lived.

I never sailed in San Pedro Harbor again, but I liked sailing enough to sign up for lessons in Marina del Rey. There were several of us. After our lessons, we gathered at a local bar for drinks. I only remember one guy, young, blond, and handsome, who drove a red pickup with a decal on the fender that said SAVE THE CHOCOLATE MOOSE, which cracked me up every time I saw it. Except for bringing cocaine to Brian's boat that one time, I was not using drugs during the time I was sailing. I believed I had found my identity again.

Even after those lessons, I still didn't know how to sail, but I wasn't aware of that yet. Mom bought me a little red sailboat, a Lido 14 named Valentine. I didn't ask her how and where she got it, because I didn't want to know the answer.

Mom invited Guy and Ron to join us on the slip where Valentine was docked to christen her over a bottle of Champagne. The Lido 14 tends to wobble, and the first time I took her out alone in the harbor, the rocking scared me. I thought Valentine would capsize and roll me into the ocean. One of the lessons I got should have been what to do when a small boat capsizes and how easy it is to get it upright again and jump back in, especially if the boat is tiny.

Terrified of my little boat, I made my way back to the dock and never sailed Valentine again. Eventually, as with other gifts from my mother, the boat just disappeared, as did sailing.

One day, Mom asked me for my credit card. I knew giving her the card was a mistake, but I was afraid to say no. I knew that Mom didn't understand how a checkbook worked. In her mind, as long as there were checks, there was money. She had a willful ignorance about money.

Before my monthly statement even arrived, I received a call from the credit card company that my card was over my limit by hundreds of dollars. I was furious. I confronted her. She didn't try to deny anything, and it was my fault anyway. I knew to never accept a check from her because it would bounce. I knew never to loan her money. I don't know why I didn't see that giving her my credit card was the same as loaning her money.

I had to harangue her for a month before she paid me back.

Ron and I were the only two people Mom ever paid back, but that's because like pit bulls, we latched on to her until she cleared her debt.

For years, my mother resented that when my brothers and I reached twenty-one, we started to receive money from our trusts. My portion was about $20,000, which I deposited in my bank. In the '70s, $20,000 was a lot of money. It infuriated my mother that she didn't have control over the money. She referred to the insurance as "my money." She never asked me for my share, but she did approach my brothers.

Guy helped her out. Ron and I were harder-edged about our mother.

Ron once told me that by the time Mom was released from prison, he no longer thought of her as his mother. It was too late for him. He had raised himself, bumping around from one friend's house to another. At sixteen, he rented an apartment with his brother and a friend and became a short order cook at a local coffee shop, where he met his future wife, Cyndy. I, on the other hand, lived in fear of everything and desperately needed to have a mother, even though I instinctively knew to protect myself against her manipulations for money or signing my name to documents on her behalf.

I understood her resentment. During her marriage, she had never worked. When she was released from prison, the state had given her $60. She had no skills. She had been incarcerated almost eight years. The world had changed. She was going to have trouble enough just learning her way in society again, much less trying to find a job with a murder conviction on her record. We never discussed it, but she must have been scared to death. All I thought about was my expectation that she would take up being my mother where she left off, only better.

Guy was her most vulnerable child, and the only one of us who gave her some of the trust money he had left. When my mother was released from prison, Guy was in dental school at Loma Linda University in California. He had taken out huge loans for school. That Guy needed to pay for his education either did not occur or matter to her. She began pestering Guy for "loans." He simply could not say no.

This was an ugly and damaging game she played with her son all through dental school. His loan check would arrive. She'd convince Guy to loan her money with a promise to pay him back with some exorbitant amount of interest. His tuition fee would come due. He'd call Mom for his money. She would promise him a check. It wouldn't come. His school would press him to pay his overdue bill. Guy would call Mom again. Since his tuition was already late, she'd assure him she would just send a check straight to the school. They always bounced. The school would notify Guy. Furious, he would call Mom again.

"I can't figure out why that happened," she would say, seeming incredulous and confused. "Just tell them to put it through again."

Sometimes it cleared, but more than once her check bounced again.

Sometimes Guy would be approaching a final exam. Instead of being able to put his energy into studying, he found himself desperately trying to reach our mother because the school was threatening that he couldn't take his finals until his bill was paid. How Guy ever made it through dental school and the state boards is beyond me.

I would have thought Mom would have some shame for how she behaved with Guy, but far from it. Instead, she reasoned with her twisted logic that by paying him back for his loans, she actually was paying for his tuition.

It was during our time in Marina del Rey that Mom was diagnosed with breast cancer. Mom found a lump in her breast and said nothing to anyone for a year. She finally asked Cyndy, who was my sister-in-law by this point, to check the lump. Alarmed by the size of the lump, Cyndy insisted Mom see a doctor right away.

When she finally had the lump biopsied, she learned she had breast cancer. Rather than go with my brothers to take Mom to UCLA Medical Center the night before her radical mastectomy, I attended my night class. I had returned to college to pursue my bachelor's in English, and I decided I would not skip school to be with her.

By the time I arrived home from school, my brothers were back at our apartment. Ron recently told me Mom wanted to stop for a flower to take to the hospital with her. The minute I walked in the door, I sensed a typical Mom fiasco unfolding. She had learned that if a will was handwritten and signed by its originator, it was legitimate, and decided my brothers needed to draw one up for her even though she had nothing to leave to anybody.

The most hurtful part of the will was that Mom was leaving Guy $1 because she claimed she had paid his way through dental school. By contract, she left everything, whatever "everything" meant, to Kimi. Her heart had never healed from losing Kimi.

CHAPTER 35:

The Con

At the same time Mom was struggling with cancer, her friend Michael, a successful businessman, convinced her she should own her own employment agency. According to Michael's calculations, they needed $75,000 to open an agency. He would invest $25,000, leaving Mom to find the rest. One of her employees at her current agency wanted in on the deal. It was agreed that each of them would pay in $25,000 to open their first office in Beverly Hills. The only problem for Mom was she had no access to $25,000. Now she needed me.

When Mom and I were living at the Mediterranean Village, a former boss of mine and her Lebanese husband had invited me to brunch at Scandia to meet their friend Akeem. Akeem and I were easy together, no shyness or awkwardness—our conversation flowed naturally. By the end of the brunch, Akeem had invited me back to his hotel (after a quick stop to his dealer's). We spent the rest of the afternoon and early evening drinking Champagne, sniffing cocaine, and getting the drift of each other without sex before he drove me home.

Akeem owned apartments and homes all over the world but not yet in Los Angeles. When he was in town, he reserved a suite at a high-end hotel in Westwood. He was from Saudi Arabia and had left there to attend USC, earning a bachelor of science and a graduate degree in chemistry. I became Akeem's Los Angeles girlfriend. When he was abroad, I dated, but when he came to town, I only wanted to be with him. He was generous and fun with a great sense of humor. His closest friends were Middle Eastern, mostly Persian. He finally bought a home in Laurel Canyon. Akeem became my lifeline for many years. We got high together and drank together, dancing with his Persian friends to Michael Jackson's *Thriller*—my favorite was "Billie Jean"—until we were completely exhausted.

Akeem encouraged me to investigate opening a boutique. I didn't see myself owning a business because my life was adrift. Given the chance to turn my life around didn't excite me so much as scare me. But Akeem never stopped offering. Finally, I told him I would like to own a bookstore. He was excited and told me to research the possibility, learn the ins and outs of such a venture, and write a proposal.

That I needed to put in the work surprised me because I didn't expect to have to do anything except show up for my opening night. Once I started my research, I found out that most bookstores folded because they couldn't compete with the big guys, like Barnes & Noble. Also, it took a lot of capital to stock a bookstore.

Akeem continued nudging me, to no avail. Every conversation about setting me up in a business made me uneasy because it confirmed my stunning lack of ambition, which made me feel worse about myself than I already did.

Akeem's continued offers caught my mother's attention, however. She recognized an opening for herself. If I lacked ambition, why not ask Akeem for a $25,000 loan to get her started in her own business? While I knew I should refuse,

I agreed—with the caveat that I wouldn't ask him on her behalf unless he made another offer to me, which I believed wouldn't happen.

Regrettably, and to my surprise, Akeem broached the subject again. I dreaded having to ask him to loan my mother money. I felt embarrassed and nervous, angry at Mom for putting me in this position and angry at myself for putting me in this position. I didn't warn him that she might not be the best risk. I thought I didn't have to because I assumed she was small fry compared to the world economy in which he played. Besides, if he had required me to supply him with a business plan, certainly he would do the same with my mom. Plus, Akeem and Mom were friends. When I was smoking his opium in my bedroom with a friend, she was making him omelets. When he held elaborate luncheons with white-gloved servers, she was always invited.

Unfortunately, the only precaution Akeem took when loaning my mother $25,000 was to have me witness a handwritten note. There was a second $25,000 check, too, but I only heard about that later.

Mom and her partners opened their employment office in Beverly Hills. They threw an expensive open house for their new office.

Flush with money, Mom bought a used red Porsche, which stalled every time I drove it. After the Porsche, she bought a black 1960s Mercedes Roadster, which also stalled regularly.

Soon she and her partners opened another office in Newport Beach. A white limousine would whisk them to Newport or roll them around Beverly Hills looking for more office space. Power lunches became part of her routine. Mom's supposed investor, Michael, played to her vanity and ambition, promising millions in profits. He kept my mom busy planning and dining, floating on a pink cloud, until the day Mom showed up to work in Beverly Hills to find the doors to her business locked and an out-of-business sign hanging on the door. She loved the schmoozing and lunches and decorating, but she didn't love the bookkeeping, leaving this in Michael's hands.

Except for the administrative part, my mother would have been a successful businesswoman. She was not lazy. She understood what it took besides money to run an employment business. Her fatal flaw was her willful ignorance about money, except to spend it. In less than a year, Michael had siphoned every bit of money from the partnership account into his private accounts. If Mom had not been struggling with cancer, she could have taken him to court, but that would have been too traumatic for her. So he stole all the money from their business with impunity.

I was with her that terrible morning when she discovered she'd been locked out of her office. I remember how beautiful she looked, tan and wearing her lavender linen dress, a wide Roman gold belt wrapped around her waist. When her key wouldn't open the door to their office, she looked over at me as though I knew what was up. When she saw the blank look on my face, she turned and walked down the hall and disappeared behind another door. I stood waiting for her.

As she came back toward me, her eyes were glazed, the blood drained from her face. I saw the shift happen. I stood frozen, watching the end of Reni Maxwell. She had been able to parlay herself into an honest and self supporting member of society after leaving prison. She had stumbled once or twice, but she had pulled herself up. She had found a career she was well suited for. She had worked hard. She had not looked back, played the victim, or sunk into despair. She had tried. She had failed.

Prison had taught my mother many things, but not, ironically, how to spot a swindler.

Whatever in her that had cared for me or anyone else drained out that day. She lifted her head slightly, her stare cold and remote. Mom was gone. She never came back. Needing to leave Marina del Rey behind her, she moved to Beverly Hills.

What did I do? I got married.

CHAPTER 36:

Sliding

Ned, the golden boy of the English department, looked like John Kennedy Jr. He'd been rejected by every university he'd applied to because he was lazy. He'd aced the SATs but earned bad grades in high school, caring only about the school literary magazine. This landed him at Cal State Northridge, where he became a straight-A student in every class, always alone and unfriendly, rather arrogant yet wowing all of us with his literary acumen and good looks.

Ned was nine years younger than I was. Twenty-nine and never married, with a string of failed relationships, it seemed better to me to have to later say I was divorced rather than to admit that no one had ever asked me to marry them. Divorce carried more status. The assumption could be that someone had wanted you to be his wife, but it just didn't work out.

I decided the best way to meet him was to ask him to help me with a poem that I didn't need help with. Right away, I could see Ned was lonely. I had failed at every relationship. We were a perfect match.

Several months later, we married. Akeem threw a bachelor party for Ned as well as supplied all the roses at our reception.

It lasted fourteen months.

During our fleeting union, Ned and I moved into a duplex in Sherman Oaks. I'd moved on from drugs for the time being. I planted flower box gardens of impatiens while Ned read Lichtenstein. He rose at 5:00 a.m. each morning to read Virgil's *Aeneid* in Latin. I dragged myself out of bed in time for my classes. He wanted to be a professor and decided I was not scholarly enough for him, which was true. He wanted a wife who also rose at 5:00 a.m. to read *Aeneid*.

Clearly, I was not that person, but I knew who was. I introduced him to Shadi, the second smartest person in the English department.

After our divorce, they got married.

Right after Ned moved out, Mom moved in with me. Her cancer was spreading, but I didn't know it at the time. She looked fragile, her eyes sad, her movements graceful. She sat on the couch in our shared apartment, drinking coffee. I loved watching her, wishing I had her femininity and elegance, even as she sat sipping coffee from an ugly mug.

We only lasted one month together due to the tension swirling between us. She moved in with Cyndy for a while, and then all over the place. It was hard to keep track of her, and I was not sober.

That time of my life is a blur. Guy, Ron, and I lived to escape our pasts and presents through reckless behavior that continued to escalate. Mimicking my mother's behavior, I became a nomad. Unable to pay my rent, I found myself panicked and paralyzed. As I had done any number of times before, I turned to a man to rescue me. This time it was John—tall and handsome, always grinning. He was Ron's best friend since childhood. We'd known each other for years and harbored a mutual crush.

Once my brothers informed John that I was about to become homeless, he called me to offer to fly his plane to pick me up and move in with him in Duarte, a dry little burg in the far reaches of Los Angeles County, hometown of playwright and actor Sam Shepard, who once described Duarte as "a strange kind of melting pot . . . Midwestern elements all jumbled together. People on the move who couldn't move anymore, who wound up in trailer parks."

I dragged Jolie, my cat, with me. John owned a golden retriever and a macaw, and between the screeching and the barking, poor Jolie lived in terror under the bed until I moved out.

John and I hadn't discussed our future, but we should have, because we didn't have the same thing in mind. He assumed I would get a job, and I assumed he would take care of me.

I hated living in the middle of nowhere. I hated John's house, dark, smelling of birdseed and bird. It turned out John and I weren't really attracted to each other.

Soon, I invited a former English professor of mine to John's for a weekend of drugs and drinking. I confessed my unhappiness, and my professor friend invited me to stay with him in Woodland Hills, a lovely place where the sweet and musty scents of the flora and fauna permeate the air. My professor friend introduced me to a friend of his who turned out to open a new path for me. She was a principal of a local elementary school and asked me if I would like to volunteer in an after-school tutoring program for underprivileged children.

I jumped at the chance. I did not consider myself a patient person when it came to little kids, but I needed to fill time until I found a job. There, I found something wonderful about myself—I loved these grade-school kids who worked so hard at their homework. I loved watching the light ignite when they figured something out. I loved the patience I found in myself, and I loved their open hearts, which opened mine. Tutoring these eight- and ten-year-old kids opened me to my future. I realized I wanted to be a teacher.

In 1984, I moved back to the Mediterranean Village and rented a single, thinking of the fun I'd had when my mother and I had lived there. Because I now knew my path, I enrolled for the fourth time at California State University in Northridge to complete my degree in English literature. I'd left Jolie with my ex-husband after leaving John's; now I retrieved her.

But I no longer belonged or felt comfortable around my old friends. Nor could I stop using drugs.

Mom found me a job working in a bank while I finished college. I was sure they wouldn't hire me, but they did. They didn't fire me, either, when I showed up for my first day of work high. The manager liked me. It was clear that I was smart, even though I made nothing but mistakes and often arrived late and dressed inappropriately.

One night, I'd been out with a friend drinking and doing cocaine. I didn't get back to my apartment until 6:00 a.m. I was exhausted and coming down from the drugs and alcohol, knowing I had to be at work by eight o'clock. I saw myself in a glass mirror as I slid to the floor, my knees pulled to my chest, scared and crying. I arrived to work late, sure I would be fired, but I wasn't.

Somehow, I managed to finish school, earning my bachelor of arts in English from Northridge. I wanted to march and receive my diploma. A friend at the bank wanted to celebrate my achievement. My graduation wasn't until that evening, and I fooled myself into thinking I could have it both ways: celebrate my accomplishment in the afternoon with my friend and attend my graduation that evening.

Once he pulled out the cocaine and Champagne, the afternoon turned into dusk, into night, into the wee hours of the morning.

I lasted at the bank only two months before I quit. I got a job bartending at the Entourage, a French restaurant in West Hollywood. The Record Plant, a famous recording studio, was next door to the restaurant. Rock stars like Rod Stewart sat at the bar drinking. It was there where I met David, the sound engineer who worked with Kiss. He stopped by the Entourage every afternoon for a few glasses of whiskey. We flirted. We became friends and lovers. By the time he had finished the album he was in town to work on, I had fallen in love with him.

I was recently divorced from Ned and finishing my bachelor's degree in English literature, working as a bartender at the Entourage restaurant next door to the world-famous Record Plant studio. The studio had been known for decades as the source of legendary albums such as the Eagles' *Hotel California* and Fleetwood Mac's *Rumours*. Proximity to this chaotic world of rock led me back to my old habits, which led to a surrealistic mix of drugs, sex, and being back in school at age thirty-one.

David lived in New York City and returned there when the album was completed. I wrote him love letters and lived for his phone calls, complaining that he wasn't calling enough. He hinted that I wrote too much. I was embarrassed and panicked that I was losing him.

I began to push him to fly me to New York. I believed that if I were with him, everything would return to the way it was in the beginning. Maybe I would stay in New York, maybe even marry him. He resisted, but I persevered, and just before Christmas, he flew me to New York. The terror of being alone caused me to push men, trying to make relationships move faster, rather than pulling back with some self-respect.

When I arrived in New York, a limousine pulled to the curb. David opened the back door, offering me Champagne and cocaine. This was exactly how I imagined it would be. He took me to a restaurant in Greenwich Village, where I ordered a hamburger dripping with béarnaise sauce. A sign hung on the wall by our booth that read WHEN YOU LEAVE NEW YORK, YOU GO NOWHERE.

David owned a co-op in Greenwich Village. When we entered his building, the doorman greeted him. An elevator operator carried us to his floor. I envisioned a swanky co-op, but when we stepped out of the elevator, the long and narrow halls felt claustrophobic, the lighting oppressive rather than atmospheric, the doors and walls a dirty white. When we entered David's apartment, stacks of newspapers posing as a carpet covered every inch of his dining room. Filled with junk, his apartment, the size of a big closet, confirmed that he was a hoarder. A tiny pathway had been carved among all his things, which led from the front door and kitchen to the bedroom. I felt everything closing in on me, a panic attack coming on. I wanted to go home. I didn't like him anymore.

Also, I had arrived in New York a different woman than the one he had left behind in Los Angeles. Sometime between his leaving Los Angeles and my arriving in New York, I had lost my ability to control cocaine. I turned out to be just as much a disappointment to David as he was to me. After several lines of cocaine, we walked around the Village until I become so paranoid, we returned to his apartment. I should have gone home that night, but instead I stayed for the full three days.

The morning I was flying back to California, we were drinking coffee at a sidewalk café.

"I guess I'll never see you again," he said.

"Why would you even want to?" I replied.

He understood.

I left New York, never to see David again.

Not long after I got back from New York, I stumbled out of the Record Plant and heard somebody running after me. It was Rose, the tough, beautiful manager and girlfriend of John Lennon's sound engineer. She knew every rock star in town because everyone recorded at the Record Plant. She drank and smoked heavily, used drugs, and managed to run the recording studio. I wanted to be Rose. But this night, she was there to deliver some tough love.

"It's not the same for you now," she said. "I hate seeing you hanging out like this. David's not here anymore. You need to stay away."

I began to cry from embarrassment.

"These people aren't your friends anymore," she said firmly.

I actually took Rose's hand and thanked her. I never returned to the studio.

When I returned to my apartment that night, Jolie jumped on my bed, but I pushed her off. Months after that, she stopped eating and began to waste away. She had cancer. I would harbor guilt for this, too. I didn't hurt her, but she was lonely and needed me, and I rejected her.

I was about to hit a new low.

Rick, a music scout I knew, invited me to his apartment on the beach off the Pacific Coast Highway. He persuaded me to try freebasing, something I had promised myself I'd never do. His upstairs neighbor sold cocaine. All he had to do was place a call and the neighbor let down a basket carrying little white packets of cocaine. It was fun watching Rick cook the powder and prepare the water pipe.

After my first hit, I slumped into the couch, lost in nirvana, the most exquisite sensation I had ever experienced. Drifting away like this was peaceful. I was willing and almost hoping death felt like this.

The sensation didn't last. Rick offered me another hit.

This cycle repeated itself until six o'clock the next morning, when suddenly Rick announced he had a meeting at Capitol Records and offered to call me a cab. I was supposed to move in with my mother again that day, and I hadn't even packed for the move. I became frantic and begged him to drop me off at home on his way.

He was angry, but he agreed.

I managed to call my mother, crying for help, confessing I had been freebasing all night and hadn't boxed up, hadn't even collected the boxes or done anything for the move. She said she'd be there in five minutes.

I curled up on my twin bed, unable to bring myself around, scared I was slipping away. Mom arrived and held me in her lap. We looked for all the world like the *Pietà*, except she wasn't Mary, and I wasn't Jesus.

Mom didn't want to take me to the emergency room because she was afraid I might be arrested.

"Are you going to make it?" she asked.

I said I would, and she folded me into the bed. I fell asleep while she packed me for the move, this time to Beverly Hills with her.

It didn't take long for Mom to regret moving me in, announcing that if I couldn't pay my share of the rent more than one time, I had to go.

I hadn't missed paying my rent. It rattled me to hear her say this.

She found plenty of fault with me. I didn't clean up my kitchen mess fast enough or well enough. If I decided to soak in the tub, she warned me not to use her unguents and to make sure I cleaned the tub. If I wanted something from her room, I needed her permission.

Then there was Frankie, a tall, curly-haired Italian with a big mustache and sad brown eyes. When I came home one night from class, he was sitting on the couch drinking wine, with his arm around my mother.

I was shocked because my mother had never dated a man younger than she was, especially someone closer to my age than to hers. I knew he was bad news even as he jumped up from the couch to shake my hand, smiling from ear to ear, and rushed to pour me a glass of wine.

When I asked Mom how she'd met him, she told me he delivered supplies to their offices in Beverly Hills, and they'd become friendly. I learned many years later, after finding a box of letters between them, that Mom had lied. Frankie was in Chino Prison at the same time Mom was in prison. I don't know how they connected, but they became prison pen pals. They must have continued writing to each other after Mom was released from prison. In that same box, I found a letter Frankie wrote thanking her for visiting him.

Frankie continued his futile efforts to win my favor. He bought me an expensive red leather hobo bag I wanted. He supplied me with cocaine.

One night, I woke up to find him lurking just outside my bedroom door. I could tell he was drunk.

I wasn't afraid of him. "Go to your own room, Frankie," I snapped.

He left.

I tried to make a big deal of this to my mom, hoping it could be the end of Frankie. I hoped her anger that this was similar to molestation might get him out of our lives, but it didn't work. She just yelled at him.

Given how much I enjoyed my volunteer experience with the underprivileged kids, I applied for a high school teaching credential. I had been smoking opium with a friend the night before the test. Once again, just as I had for job interviews, I jeopardized my future, setting myself up to fail the test. I didn't put myself in these positions because I was nervous. I knew showing up high for appointments that were important to me for a job or a test or whatever was detrimental to my future. My problem was that I was partying all the time and not thinking of my future.

Somehow, I passed the test to get into the credential program, and thanks to a wonderful woman named Rita, a former nun, I began working at the UCLA Research Library as a clerk while attending night school.

Even though I was moving my life forward, my drug use kept me on the edge of failure all of the time. But Rita believed in me, believed I would straighten out. I had managed to graduate, and I was enrolled in a credential program, but my behaviors hadn't changed.

Usually late, I often arrived in torn T-shirts or plunging necklines, still high and with little interest in my job except to get through the day. Terry, the office manager for all of the administrative assistants, complained of my poor work habits. Rita talked to me, reminding me that while I worked for her, I also worked for Terry. It did little good. I resented Terry because I was more educated than she was, and I didn't want anyone telling me what to do except Rita.

I drove Terry crazy. Rita protected me.

One of the administrative assistants edited the library newsletter and lived with her boyfriend, a postdoc in chemistry. I envied her. I wanted her job. I wanted to write the library newsletter. I wanted to live with a boyfriend working on his postdoctoral program in chemistry. I told myself that if I had a great job like hers, everything about me would change—I would dress appropriately. I would arrive early. I would stay late. I would never miss a day of work.

Instead, I arrived one morning in cutoff jeans and a T-shirt that kept sliding off my shoulders. The newsletter editor's boss complained to Rita.

This resulted in Rita having to talk to me yet again. Just as I always did, I apologized to Rita, promising to clean up my act.

Finally, everyone but Rita encouraged the director of the library to fire me. Counting on me to charm him, Rita sent me in to talk to him and save my job, which is what happened. Even though I was an unreliable mess, people found me funny, someone with an unusual take on life, often spilling out what other people were thinking but couldn't say out loud. I also flirted with everyone—male, female, married, or single. To some in the library, I was a refreshing novelty. And Rita never gave up on me.

One of the requirements for earning my credential was to observe and be mentored by a high school English class for a semester and teach a lesson at the end of the term. Rita encouraged me to call Marymount High School, an all-girls' school on Sunset Boulevard across the street from the Research Library, to observe a class. I did, and an English teacher agreed to mentor me.

I remained negligent in all aspects of my life except for observing this English class. I never missed a class. I arrived early. I asked questions, took notes, and listened to and absorbed everything. The girls liked me. My past looked nothing like theirs, nothing like anyone I'd ever known, but it had given me an irreverent view of the world that was appealing to teenage girls.

At the end of the term, I had to teach the class. I had completed my methods class and knew how to prepare an imaginary lesson plan, but the thought of devising a plan I would actually teach worried me.

Because my lesson had to be completed by the end of one class, I chose the short story "The Gift of the Magi," by O. Henry. I loved this story about a young husband and wife who sacrifice something precious to them in order to buy their beloved a gift to complement the other's precious item. The wife cuts and sells her hair to buy a gold fob for her husband's watch, and he sells his watch to buy her two beautiful combs for her hair.

My plan wasn't deep or sophisticated, but the girls engaged with me—a relief because students can make or break a teacher—and by the time class ended, I felt euphoric. It was new for me to feel not a drug-induced euphoria, but a high that came from being prepared, connecting with the girls, and feeling pride in my work.

With a sense of direction, finally, I started to make some changes in my life.

CHAPTER 37:

Done

Grace arrived, but not immediately. Although I did move to Venice Beach, away from my mother and her thug boyfriend, Frankie, I continued using drugs. I found a single half a block from the Venice Boardwalk in Venice Beach. The price was right, and I jumped at the chance. Mom practically furnished my whole place with a navy-blue futon, wicker bookcases, a chest, and an elephant side table.

I hung blue flowered curtains and a clear bathroom curtain with red polka dots. I bought a baby-blue faux vintage telephone. I lined up all my books on the wicker bookcases and pushed my grandfather's cherrywood secretary desk against the wall. All of this to complement a hideous burnt-orange carpet. But that didn't matter. This was my home, my womb.

Not long after I moved in, Mom came roaring into our parking lot in a little red Triumph. I thought she'd bought a new car. I was wrong. She wanted to give me the car and carry the pink slip. I drove a broken-down Honda, so I wanted the Triumph, and this was in keeping with my mom's way of being—spoiling me and buying things I couldn't afford. The problem was that she really couldn't afford the things she gave me either.

I was never honest with myself about this issue, never willing to admit I shouldn't let Mom buy me anything. Fortunately, I was wary of this cute little Triumph, which I knew had most likely been stolen by Frankie.

I don't believe Mom was setting me up on purpose. She had lived in red alert for so long, she didn't even notice. So I didn't get mad. Instead, I informed her, "You realize that me taking on the pink slip would be bad news for me, right?"

She seemed surprised.

Venice Beach was perfect for me, a combination of ratty and charming old buildings mixed with new modern condos, evidence of the creeping gentrification. Venice was and still is a little seedy. I lived on Navy Street, the dividing line between Santa Monica and Venice. The moment I moved to Venice, I knew I never wanted to leave. Almost everything was either a walk or a bike ride away. My neighbors were mostly my age, and everyone either bought or sold drugs or both.

I often spent my afternoons grading essays at the Rose Café or at my desk, door open so I could smell the salt air and feel the ocean breeze.

One Friday afternoon not long after I moved in, I sat with my door open grading papers when my neighbor Tom leaned against my doorpost and said, "I'd like to invite you to my place for libations when you're finished working."

"Okay," I replied, then had to look up the definition of libations when he left.

When I finished my work, I walked the two doors down. His door was open. When I entered the apartment late that afternoon, it was dark but neat. He invited me to sit down at his table; he offered me a line of coke. I hadn't used cocaine since I'd moved in. As the evening wore on, Tom and I continued drinking while he offered me line after line of cocaine.

It must have been four or five in the morning when Tom folded his packet of cocaine and set it aside. He stared at me and said, "There's plenty more where that came from, but now I want a little something in return."

The most wonderful thing happened to me in that moment. I was so furious, I was fearless. I stood up and announced, "If you want me to sleep with you for more cocaine, it's not going to happen. I'm not attracted to you."

I stumbled home, plopped on my bed, and fell asleep.

Tom never made a pass at me again. In fact, a few weeks later when one of his buddies tried to press me to go with them to buy drugs and I declined, Tom intervened, saying, "When she says no, she means no, guys. Leave her alone."

I wish I could have had better boundaries around my drug use, but I didn't. Tom's dealer lived in Venice several blocks away. He was a tall, bald Black man who lived in a white clapboard house on a street with very few streetlights. On the day Tom introduced me to him, a rail-thin blonde, eyes sunken into her skull, opened the door and directed us down the hall to a room. Tom later told me she was a prostitute, the dealer her pimp. She was not allowed in the room with us as we sniffed up a few lines before making our purchase. I imagined the horror of being that poor girl in the other room, completely at this guy's mercy. I couldn't help thinking about the girl, about how easily that could be me, how horrible it would be for someone to have that kind of power over me. I began feeling nervous and wanted to get out of there.

Tom noticed my discomfort, and we left quickly.

I had a strong will but understood that continuing to do drugs would strip away that resolve. I couldn't let that happen.

CHAPTER 38:

Nearing the End

I lost track of my mother for most of the last year and a half of her life. As her cancer advanced, my brothers and I rarely knew where she was. Then suddenly, she'd pop up.

During one of her appearances, I found myself driving with her in her clunky blue Oldsmobile, smoke puffing out of the tailpipe. She had been out of touch for months. Frankie had gotten involved in running cocaine to Hawaii, and her part in the enterprise was following the person delivering the drugs to the buyers, making sure the delivery had been made. She tried to rope me into the scheme, telling me it was a great opportunity for me, lots of money and free trips to Hawaii. She also assured me that it was completely safe since the person carrying the cocaine had no idea they were being followed; if something should go wrong, the person packing the cocaine would be busted, not me.

I was incredulous about her offer. All I saw was prison time or death.

After I declined, I didn't see her again for another two months.

The next time Mom called me, she told me to meet her at a motel in the upscale neighborhood Brentwood. She gave me directions and told me I couldn't tell anyone.

I didn't ask questions. I drove to meet her at the motel, tucked in a tiny dell off Sunset Boulevard looking nothing like it belonged in Brentwood. She met me in the parking lot. We sat and talked in my car.

I did not see Frankie. I felt bad that Mom was living in a motel. She didn't ask anything of me. She just wanted to talk. There was nothing memorable about our conversation.

Then, once again, she vanished.

When Mom surfaced again, it was to inform her children she had bought a home with Frankie in Simi Valley. Feeling settled and loving animals, Mom bought a black Chow named Bear that ended up practically tearing her arm off and had to be put down, which broke her heart.

My brothers and I visited her once there. Her dream of having Kimi with her had finally come true. But Kimi was a teenager, not a little girl anymore, and her bond with her mother was fragile. They really didn't know each other. Kimi asked Mom if her boyfriend, who wore a chicken leg hanging from his earlobe, could stay at the house. Wanting Kimi to be happy, Mom agreed, but the boyfriend's sulkiness, messiness, and general disrespectfulness made Mom angry. She told Kimi she wanted her to stay but the boyfriend had to go. Kimi left with her boyfriend, and I couldn't blame her. My mother had never been a mother to her.

After Kimi left, Mom made a tape recording addressed to future grandchildren. In the video, she sits next to the fireplace in a black kaftan with silver trim holding a glass of white wine. She talks into the camera. She does not say anything bad about her life. She talks about her father taking her sledding when they lived in Canada. She wants her future grandchildren to love her, to know that she was happy and had loved life.

I wish that her story had ended as that fairy tale she was creating on that day. But the home slipped into foreclosure. Frankie disappeared. Mom claimed she had turned him over to the Florida corrections facility from which he had supposedly escaped.

Then Mom once more disappeared as well.

For the last year of her life, no one in my family knew where Mom was living, and later, no one would remember how she'd arrived at Ron's apartment. But when I found out she was there on Christmas Eve, I immediately drove from Venice to Redlands.

Guy and Ron, along with a few of their childhood friends, were well on their way to debauchery when I arrived. Mom sat wearing the white silk kaftan Akeem had given her and watched us. She was quiet, but I failed to think anything about it as I climbed as high as possible, inhaling cocaine and nitrous oxide, drinking gin and tonics, and chain-smoking until four in the morning. In my pocket, I carried a Valium that I intended to swallow in order to sleep.

When Mom told me she wasn't feeling well and hoped she could sleep, I saw that she was pale, her eyes sunken and sad. I pulled the Valium out of my pocket and handed it to her, knowing that without it I would thrash around that night, wide awake, anxiety and fear roiling through me, before finally drifting into an uneasy sleep.

When Mom's children stumbled downstairs in the early afternoon on Christmas Day, we discovered that she had decorated and been cooking Christmas dinner all morning. She was still wearing the white silk kaftan, the house smelled of turkey, and the table was set and decorated for Christmas.

We sat silently, exhausted, hung over, and dry-mouthed, trying to eat Mom's dinner that she had worked so hard on. She knew this would be her last Christmas dinner with us. We knew her cancer had returned, but we were too estranged from her to understand this. All she wanted was one more Christmas with us, but none of us could verbalize what we were experiencing. We were too far gone into our own worlds from years of not connecting, from years of never discussing our feelings, and years of reeling from disappointment and loss.

CHAPTER 39:

Not Even a Goodbye

A little more than a month after Christmas, on Tuesday, January 28, 1986, the space shuttle *Challenger* exploded seventeen seconds after takeoff, killing the seven astronauts aboard, including teacher Christa McAuliffe, whose students were among the millions watching the launch. On that fateful day, I was called to UCLA Medical Center to be with Mom. I walked there from Marymount.

She was in a little room all alone, sitting on the bed. It was dark, her arms wrapped around her, rocking in pain. I had been with her twenty minutes, and not one nurse or doctor had come to help her. I couldn't bear to see her suffering.

I ran down the hall screaming, "What is wrong with you people, my mother is in unbearable pain and nobody has come to help her!" I started crying. "Somebody help her! Somebody help her!"

Finally, a nurse approached me and told me I would have to leave if I continued to cause such a ruckus. In less than five minutes, the nurse returned and hooked Mom up to a morphine drip until they could attend to her.

Later that year, I met Mom at a Medicaid facility in the San Fernando Valley for her radiation treatment. This only happened once. She was dressed expensively, a $400 Gucci bag hanging off her shoulder. We laughed at the irony. I waited in the waiting room and wouldn't remember anything about how she got out or the status of her health.

Because everyone was so disconnected, I did not know that Mom had moved to Redlands to live with Cyndy, who was at this point separated from my brother Ron. Mom had lost her green card. Born in Canada, she'd never become an American citizen. Cyndy was trying to help her get a new one and had begun driving her from Redlands to the Valley, which is a long way, for her radiation treatments.

Mom lived with her about a month. Eventually, though, it became too difficult for Mom to climb Cyndy's stairs. Then one day, out of nowhere it seemed to me, she was no longer at Cyndy's.

By then, I knew her cancer had metastasized to her bones and liver. She looked tired and bloated the next time I saw her. I was in denial. I thought she was going to beat the cancer and our family would come together again.

I was now working as a teacher at Marymount. I told her what a good mom she had been and that I wanted her to see Marymount's chapel, the carved beam ceiling and the stained-glass windows telling the story of Christ's life. She asked me to be patient with her if she couldn't make it. I remember feeling fearful that she might never see Marymount. But I could not see that she was dying in front of me. All the years of dysfunction and deception left me unable to offer her anything except to say, "That's okay."

We eventually learned that Mom was living with a former employee and friend, Layla, and her family in the high desert. Ron and Cyndy and Guy and I drove there and found her in a dark laundry room, asleep on a mattress, suffering alone. She was essentially homeless, bartering our family's remaining furniture for a place to sleep. We should have taken her with us when we left, but she didn't ask and we didn't offer.

Several months later, in October 1986, Ron received a call from a man in the San Fernando Valley who said, "It's time to pick up your mother." We had no idea who this man was, and Ron called me and told me to meet them at Guy's apartment the next day. Guy and Ron drove to the address the stranger had given her to pack up her belongings and drive her to Guy's apartment.

All my bedroom furniture was at that house where she had been staying, and she left it all behind. All Ron took was my mother, her clothes, and her jewelry.

I drove out to Guy's apartment that afternoon. This was the last time I would see Mom alive. When I arrived, Guy's garage door was open, and I saw Mom's beautiful clothes hanging on a metal rack. Before going up to the apartment, I checked them out as though I were at a garage sale. I rummaged through a few boxes and picked out the pieces of jewelry and clothing I planned to take home with me. I understood she wouldn't need her clothes anymore.

Was I really so hardened? Or was my indifference inevitable given that she had had such a profound, destructive effect on my life? Clothes had always been our connection. This was what she had to give, and in the end, clothes were what I had to take.

In a shoebox, I found a few big chunky rings and a squash blossom. I recognized this jewelry as Sandy's and figured Mom must have borrowed it. I always gave Mom the benefit of the doubt.

Satisfied, I climbed the stairs to Guy's apartment. There

she was, propped up against the arm of Guy's couch, an angel in that white kaftan, her blue eyes sad and looking exhausted. Guy did not want her to remain with him, so Ron had agreed to take her home with him.

My brothers had left to go to the market for food. I pulled up a chair on the other side of the coffee table. Mom told me she was just gathering her strength at Guy's for a while until she could go to Mexico for Laetrile treatment, which had gained notoriety in the 1970s and which ultimately was debunked.

"Ron's going to take me," she said. "It's all arranged."

I willfully overlooked the fact that my mother was heavily drugged and needed to sleep. I wanted her to talk to me, about me, about my life. I sat on a hardback chair on the other side of the coffee table. I remember thinking it was vain and trivial to steer the conversation to me, but I did it anyway, asking her about my tumultuous love life and if she thought the fireman would come back to me. She said she thought he would but it would be too late because I would have moved on, which is exactly what happened.

On that day, I needed to say goodbye. I didn't.

Ron, Guy, and their friends later moved Mom into Ron's house. Ron shared with me how they had to carry her in a sheet like a stork carrying a baby from its beak because she was in so much pain she could not bear to be touched. She lived about two months believing Ron would drive her to Mexico for Laetrile treatment, which she was sure would cure her, even though Ron told her she was too weak and too sick to make a trip to Mexico and reminded her that Laetrile did not cure cancer.

Mom asked Ron to find Frankie. He refused. He had caused enough trouble in our lives.

She never asked for me.

Lucille Marie Blanche Maxwell Miller, aka Reni Maxwell, died November 4, 1986, Ron and Cyndy standing beside her bed, holding her hand and kissing her cheek, as she left us. Guy and I were not there.

This is what it costs. I never said goodbye. I could not be there because I did not want my mother to curse me on her deathbed the way my grandmother had cursed her.

Grandmother Tubby, who appeared so generous with my mother upon her release from prison, buying her a car and helping my mom get a new place to live, turned out to be controlling and manipulative. My grandmother was only focused on what she wanted, which was to hold on to Kimi and keep my mother close. When my mother insisted on living her own life, a chasm opened between them. It grew so wide and was filled with so much resentment and anger that as my mother stood beside Tubby's hospital bed, tears rolling down her cheeks, her heart filled with regret and sorrow, Tubby turned to her only child and hissed, "I hope you die in as much pain and as alone as I am."

My mother obliged her.

I was sitting in front of my mirror in my little bungalow in Venice getting ready for work when the phone rang. At that early hour, I knew what it meant. I lifted the receiver to my ear. Guy, solemn but not crying, said, "Mom died just a few minutes ago."

"Oh," I mumbled.

I didn't know what else to say, and Guy didn't either.

We briefly discussed what would happen and then hung up. I called my school and told them I needed to miss my first class because I'd just received a call that my mother had died. The receptionist was incredulous that I was planning to come to work at all, but I didn't know what else to do. I didn't feel grief. I felt numb, maybe relieved. I didn't want to think about my mother. Showing up to work seemed the best thing for me.

Once I arrived, I drifted through the day in an altered state. Everyone thought I was so brave, so responsible to come to work. I thought so too. It didn't occur to me that something was wrong. It wouldn't occur to me for several more years. I thought I had meant to get out to see Mom one last time. I just never seemed to find the time.

The truth was I had never intended to go.

CHAPTER 40:

Mom's Funeral

It wasn't exactly a funeral. Our mother had been cremated, and the potluck memorial was at Ron's house. He and I had picked up her ashes from a local mortuary a few days earlier. At the time, we were planning to spread her ashes in the ocean. We wanted some kind of ritual or ceremony, a formal way to say goodbye, but nothing religious.

On the way home, with Mom riding on my lap in a cardboard box, Ron and I talked about how tossing her ashes into the ocean would be a kind of celebration, not celebrating her death, just celebrating her. She had always loved the ocean. So we ended up driving around looking for a party store. Ten minutes later, we emerged from one carrying a bag full of balloons with BON VOYAGE printed on them. We were laughing, rehearsing our speeches to Mom. It was irreverent. I didn't feel sad, or perhaps I was masking it. Our laughter a way to avoid a pain too huge to bear or if we were just done, relieved our life with her was over.

Her friends and former colleagues were shocked that there was no formal funeral. They wanted a memorial to say goodbye. Instead, we only planned the potluck.

I was one of the last ones to arrive, dressed in my mother's clothes, her jewelry, including two of her wedding rings and a thick wooden bracelet. Slung over my shoulder was her Gucci bag.

I drifted down the sidewalk to Ron's porch. Mom's friends were huddled in small groups or sitting on the cement wall of the porch sipping wine. I could hear Honey, a plump, middle-aged former colleague of Mom's, saying, "Poor Reni," as she leaned in closer to her pals, her voice dropping as I approached the group. "Had to sell her fur coat, you know."

What fur coat? My mind drifted to my mother's closet. I didn't remember any fur coat. I had never liked Honey much.

She turned around as I was walking up the steps and said, "I have your mother's sterling, collateral for the money she owed me, but I'm giving it to you anyway."

I was stunned. I was still trying to work out that fur coat, and now Honey was telling me that she had my mother's silverware? I nodded and continued into the house.

I had not brought anything for the potluck. My mom's friends and colleagues were busy in the kitchen. Ron's dining room table was filled with food.

The cardboard box that contained Mom sat on the fireplace mantel with a picture of her taken while she was in prison resting against it. The picture was taken one Christmas. The prison had set up a simple backdrop, with tree ornaments and a little Christmas holly decorating a table where she sat, wearing a white sleeveless sweater someone in prison had knitted for her. Her hands were crossed in front of her on the table, the gold rings I was now wearing glistening in the camera light, her long nails painted pearly pink. Mom's head was tilted to the left, her hair up in a French twist with curls at the top. She was looking directly at the camera. Her face looked tiny, the lines of her mouth turned down, distinct as a marionette's. Her deep-set blue eyes looked sad. This had been all she could give us that Christmas.

I kept staring at the photograph. Now I could see more than just sadness in her eyes. It was like staring at one of those deceptive pictures that could be either a vase or a woman's profile, depending on how it's viewed. My mother's face was simply pretty at first glance, but when I looked closer, she looked angry, her face tight with tension. I couldn't tear myself away from the photograph. We hadn't even bothered to put it in a nice frame.

Everything about this potluck felt sloppy and phony to me. Most of the people weren't even interacting with Guy, Ron, and me. They didn't like us much, viewing us as ingrates who had deserted their mom, leaving her racked with cancer to live at a stranger's house.

I stood by the fireplace looking at everyone and realized there wasn't a person in Ron's house to whom Mom hadn't owed money.

It also was notable who wasn't there. Cecile, a childhood friend from Canada. At some point during her trial, my mother had ordered that our piano be given to Cecile. It must have been collateral for a loan. I didn't know the story but knew that once Mom had come home from prison, things hadn't gone well with Cecile.

Then there were the Lances, the family who had opened their hearts and home to us during my mother's trial. They hadn't been invited. None of us had spoken to them in years. I didn't even know where they lived or where their grown children lived.

Darlene, a friend of my mom's since college, was there and in charge. She had always intimidated me. She was too perfect. Her hair was prematurely gray and her face was deeply lined, but she was beautiful. Her blue eyes sparkled. She always wore deep-red lipstick and her gray hair in a kind of soft curled bob. She was thin, stylish, and always immaculately dressed. Her voice was soft and breathy. I felt like an oaf around her. She lived in a beautifully decorated Mediterranean-style home in the hills of Riverside. I saw her gliding in and out of the kitchen, an apron tied around her little black dress. I was certain Mom had hit her up for money, too, but Darlene was too gracious and proper to hold any outstanding debts against my mother.

Rita was there, my boss at UCLA who had been so instrumental in getting me sober. My mother had taken Rita for more than $20,000. The first time, she was simply one of Mom's victims, another unsuspecting soul charmed and then fleeced by my mother. When I learned that she had "loaned" my mother money, I told her she would never see that money again.

"But we have it in writing," she insisted.

"Putting something in writing doesn't mean anything to my mother," I answered.

When my mother hit her up again and Rita went for it, I had to wash my hands of the whole business.

As I looked around the room, I couldn't believe these people were actually here to grieve the loss of my mother, and it wasn't just because they were never going to get their money back. They had loved her, been caught in her spell, believed she was innocent of murdering my father, and now that she was gone, they missed her. She had made each one of them believe they were her best friend and that they were the most fascinating, fabulous person in the world. And now here they all were. Who was going to make them feel better than they were now? Maybe if there had been life coaches at that time, my mother wouldn't have been fleecing everyone but just charging them a fee, using a pay scale commensurate with their ability to pay.

I felt sick inside being there at my brother's. I didn't want to be with any of these people, and they weren't exactly knocking themselves out to be with me either. Just as at any party that isn't going well, people clustered in groups of familiarity, keeping to themselves and those they knew. I knew everyone, but I wasn't interested in any of them.

I made my way to the buffet table, where I forked a few pieces of ham, scooped up the potato salad, moving down the line of dishes, filling my plate with my favorites. My body was present, but my mind was elsewhere. I walked back to the living room to keep Mom's ashes company. No one seemed to find it particularly appetizing to pick at their food and make polite conversation in this room.

I sat by myself thinking back and back. We had lost everything—our father, our mother, our home. Guy, Ron, and I were different from everyone we knew. We had slugged it out. All three of us now believed we could move on, find our path.

There were no photos of Mom around the house, no guest book to sign, no tributes to her or any kind of ceremony. There was nothing about this occasion that focused on her.

On the way back to the living room I saw Ron and Sandy in Ron's bedroom, sitting cross-legged on the bed. Even though it was daylight, the room was dark. I wandered in and joined them on the bed.

"Hi, Doobs," Sandy greeted me.

She was catching up on Ron's life. I just sat and listened. Nothing in the room looked familiar. I wondered where Ron's childhood maple bedroom set had gone. All our bedroom furniture had made it as far as the Lances' house when we moved in with them, but my brother's furniture had never moved out with him.

"I found some of your jewelry Mom borrowed," I told Sandy.

"What was it? Do you remember what it was?" she asked.

"Oh, some of your rings and the squash blossom." I tried to remember all of what was in the box.

Sandy adjusted her posture and lit up. "That stuff's all part of the inventory," she said.

"What inventory?" I inquired.

"You don't know about the robbery?" Sandy asked.

Ron and I both perked up.

"What robbery?" I asked. "What are you talking about?"

"I always knew it was your mother," Sandy said, "and this proves it." She seemed in shock or distracted. She began telling us the story as we all shifted ourselves on Ron's bed.

"Maybe you didn't know that your mother lived with me for a while in my house in Beverly Glen. That was fine. She didn't live with me long. After she moved out, she called me and wanted to borrow some money. I told her I didn't have any extra money at the moment. She didn't believe me, and it made her mad."

Mom had never been angry at Sandy, but I remembered that a year or so earlier, she had said to me, "Sandy's changed."

"How?" I'd asked.

"Her success and money have gone to her head," Mom had said at the time. "She is selfish and greedy. You can't trust her. Watch yourself."

I knew my mom sometimes tried to turn people against each other. Sandy had become a well-known and successful doctor. I did not like hearing that Sandy, whom I had known my whole life, who had loved Guy, Ron, and me, taken us for weekends all the years Mom was gone, was someone I couldn't trust. But I also knew my mother to be unreliable, and as usual, she wouldn't give me the details "to spare" me. I had learned that when she refused to give evidence of her claims, it meant the details would have uncovered her own culpability. Yet my mother had a way of making me doubt myself, distrust my own judgment.

In Ron's bedroom, sitting in a lotus pose, Sandy told Ron and me the details.

"Your mother was right," Sandy said. "I could have given her money, but I was tired of giving her money. She always promised to pay it back, give me a note, but you know . . . she never did. Not long after your mother left, there was a robbery at my house. My fur coat and some of my jewelry were taken, the very jewelry you told me your mom has."

Lacy, Sandy's Doberman, protected her house with all her might. No one except someone with a familiar scent and voice got by Lacy. Lacy knew my mom and would have wiggled her butt and wagged her tail, following Mom from room to room, as she burgled Sandy's house.

"It had to be your mother," Sandy said, laughing. "Lacy would have let your mother in the house."

Sandy said she had gone out to visit Mom in the San Fernando Valley not long before my brothers brought her to Guy's apartment. "Your mother was in a lot of pain. I helped her to the bathroom. It was awful. When I got her back in bed, I sat beside her. I knew she wasn't going to live much longer. I thought she might want to clear her burdens, so I said, 'You know I've always loved you. You're very sick. It won't matter to me, but I'm asking you if you and Frankie robbed my house.'"

Sandy said Mom just laid there with her eyes closed and never moved. She asked a few more times, gently prodding her, but Mom never responded. Sandy said she left that night and never saw Mom again.

I sat on Ron's bed, stunned. *If she could take one secret to her grave, why not another?*

This was not the first time I had thought about Mom's guilt or innocence regarding my father's death. I hadn't any doubt that she was innocent until I started living with her, and even then, I believed in her most of the time. I knew people who believed she was guilty, but I never became defensive.

Sitting on Ron's bed with Sandy, learning of the robbery, the secret she never gave up, my view of my mother slowly and painfully came into focus.

I will never know for sure. The three people—Harold, Joan Lance, and Sandy—who were with Mom immediately after the accident believed she was innocent.

I want her to be guilty. I need her to be guilty, because at least that way her suffering is somehow justifiable.

CHAPTER 41:

Cleaning Up

I began working at Marymount in the fall of 1985. Soon I was attending Friday morning mass. Marymount's chapel, with its stained-glass windows telling the story of Jesus and his disciples, its carved wood beam ceiling, its marble altar, awed and soothed me. I sat in a pew gazing at the most beautiful and largest stained-glass window above the podium portraying a scene of a saint, the cast of the soft light of the morning sun across the room enhancing the story in colors of purple and turquoise, greens and blues.

I was no longer a religious person, but I loved singing The Lord's Prayer as we held hands raising our arms, tears welling. I did not need to believe to be touched and moved in the moment. I love rituals. I loved sharing a pew with my colleagues. As a non-Catholic, I could not hold the chalice and sip the wine or have the host placed on my tongue, but I could and did cross my arms across my chest for a blessing from Father Joe.

During that first year at Marymount, I led two lives. One was being a professional, put-together teacher and the other was being a drug addict.

One week into my summer break, I was at a bar in Malibu with my neighbor Ava. A guy I'd gone out with a couple of times who lived in Malibu joined us and invited us back to his place with a couple of his friends. Everything was fine until the drugs ran out. I panicked. I couldn't fall asleep, and he shoved a glass of water and some antihistamines at me so I would shut up.

A couple of hours later, everyone was up. I felt strung out and sick. I wanted to get out of there. Ava and I climbed into her yellow Volkswagen Beetle and headed up the Pacific Coast Highway back to Venice. She told me she had more coke at her place. That was all I could think of.

Just as we reached Topanga Canyon, her car began to sputter and slow. We were out of gas. Ava had to hike up Topanga Canyon to find a gas station. It was hot that day, and even with the windows down, I was sweltering, sticky, and scared. I started to cry. I was in a panic and even considered walking home, which was ridiculous. I needed a few more lines to tide me over.

At that moment, in that stifling car by myself, I envisioned a fork in my road. One path led to a strung-out, gaunt blond woman curled up on the floor in a drug dealer's house. I saw me on that floor. I saw losing everything and wanting to die. The other path led back to Marymount. The principal believed in me. My students saw me as a real teacher whom they liked, not a drug addict. I was close to my colleagues, especially those in the English department. I loved teaching. As sorry as my life was, I was a good teacher.

I understood the future I wanted began with sobriety. I saw my choices as life or death. A voice in my head repeated an AA bromide: "You never have to feel this way again." I believed it. I chose life. I knew I was done. I didn't even feel jumpy or sick anymore.

The next thing I knew, Ava was pouring gas into her tank and we were on our way. When we got home, I went straight to my apartment and slept the rest of the day.

I got sober on June 23, 1986.

I was thirty-six years old, and I would work at Marymount for the next thirty years.

Postscript

Kimi Kai Miller died when she was twenty-five years old of a rare form of lung cancer, leaving behind two small children, Megan and Austen. She paid the greatest price of us all. She only outlived our mother by five years. And I hardly knew her.

My first memory of Kimi is of a tiny bundle lying on her back on a pink blanket on the floor of the Lances' living room. It was early in the morning, a shaft of early sunlight, a streak across the carpet. Joan Lance, still in her burgundy bathrobe, had positioned her on the floor as I tiptoed across the entryway to see my baby sister. I was sitting on my haunches examining her pretty little newborn face, her blue eyes. Her face meant everything to me. She looked like us, important to me because of the rumors that she was Arthwell Hayton's child. Even though the Lances were already guardians of my brothers and me, increasing their family to eight, I wanted to ask them to be Kimi's guardian, too. I was only fourteen, but I longed to take care of her as both sister and mother. She represented my hope. I desperately needed to keep her with us, a new adoring family, a better family; her life could be different from ours.

Her adoption, the finality, meant no more Miller family.

Mom's conviction took Kimi away from us. A cousin of Mom's wanted to adopt Kimi, with a caveat that she should never know she had been adopted. I couldn't bear the thought of losing Kimi, of Kimi never knowing she had a sister and two brothers. That just couldn't happen. It was a frontal attack on me, reality slapping me in the face, and so I begged Mom not to let the adoption happen. I had named her Kimi Kai. She was my Kimi.

I wanted her to be with us, so my grandparents took Kimi instead.

But for that baby's sake, we should have let her go. I was living a fantasy of a little girl loved and spoiled by her mother and siblings, a precious gift binding her family together.

I take myself back to that beautiful baby on the blanket. I'm still looking deeply into her pretty blue eyes. She is looking back at me, trying to convey that we needed to let her go, give her the chance to live a happy and fulfilled life.

We made a terrible mistake.

At first, Kimi was close by. My grandparents moved from Portland, Oregon, to Loma Linda, California, to raise her and make sure she knew her mother.

My mom loved Kimi, cooed over her when Grandmother Tubby or my brothers and I took her to visit. We all adored her. I loved to pretend I was her mother in a shopping mall one afternoon.

In a letter to Sandy, Mom wrote, "Kim is precious huh? . . . Deb is mad about her, which is wonderful."

More than anything, Mom wanted her parents, her children, and Sandy to move in together, like a compound where all of us would live together. It was not to be. Instead, my grandparents moved back to Portland. In a letter, Mom wrote, "I love her so terribly and hate to have her leave.

I've cried and still haven't emptied the supply. I look at her darling picture and could just die. I can't stand to see her go."

On June 21, the summer solstice, the longest day of the year, Mom said goodbye to Kimi.

Giving up her child, even though it was to her parents, had a devastating effect on my mom. It was one more blow among the many throughout her life that hardened her.

Kimi came and went from our lives quickly. My grandparents left the country after taking her in, and we didn't see her again for three or four years, not until my grandparents returned to the United States and moved back to Loma Linda. By then, Kimi and Mom were strangers, and Kimi didn't seem to know any of us. It seemed as though no one had talked to her about her siblings or shown her pictures of us.

During that visit, my grandmother invited me along with a few of her Adventist friends for dinner at her house in Loma Linda. We all sat round my grandmother's cherrywood dining table, a lace tablecloth placed on top of a protective plastic liner, her Royal Albert Petit Point china poised on her lace cloth.

During dinner, Kimi crawled under the table. My grandmother kept telling her to come out from under the table, even though Kimi was sitting quietly. As my grandmother's voice became more irritated, the atmosphere grew tense. I felt pressed to carry out the will of the table. My frustration was at their provincial way of dealing with children, their "spare the rod, spoil the child" mentality. Channeling the energy of the table in my behavior onto Kimi, I dragged her crying and screaming to her bedroom. Sitting on her bed, I pulled her into my lap, folded her into me, and rocked her back and forth as I sobbed. I kissed her face. I told her it was all right, but I was no comfort to her. She stopped crying but didn't hug me back. I'm ashamed of my actions now. She felt safe under the table.

After my grandmother's death, Kimi was sent across the country to live with a cousin, a Seventh-day Adventist who had once bragged to me how strict they were with their two children. I knew what that meant. It made me shudder. This cousin had loved my mom but had zero empathy for or understanding of Kimi. What my sister faced was a strict, unsympathetic atmosphere created by the worst kind of Adventists.

When Kimi finally moved back to California, when she was about sixteen, she moved in with the Rosamonds, who lived a block away from my grandmother's house, a lovely family whose youngest daughter was Kimi's best friend. I visited, and it was clear she was happy there.

In the early '80s, during the time I was living with Mom in Marina del Rey, I celebrated a birthday that Kimi attended. I was aware that she felt out of place. She mostly sat on the couch by herself, and I didn't make any effort to include her. I must have been in an alcohol- and drugs-induced haze, because the only thing I remember is an incident concerning the cocaine. After some of us had done a few lines, and fearing we would never stop, I screwed the black cap on the amber vial and stored it in my medicine cabinet. After dinner and cake, I returned to the bathroom to retrieve the cocaine from the cabinet. It was gone. I panicked. We all needed to finish the rest of that cocaine. I was crazy angry. Who even knew where I put it? No one, but it was gone.

I returned to the party to see if by chance someone knew where it was and had retrieved it. I was going to be okay with this; at least I would still have my cocaine. No one fessed up, and in a fury, I went after Kimi, blaming her for stealing it.

Her face was stricken. "I've never used cocaine or even seen cocaine," she whimpered.

Feeling so hateful, I screamed, "You're a liar!"

She was petrified of me. I watched her sink away. That baby's eyes had warned me many years ago as she lay on the blanket at the Lances that we needed to let her go. It didn't soften me. I didn't apologize—not ever. The incident ruined the evening. I found out later that Kimi was not the one who had stolen the drugs. I had been my very worst self, and I never made it right.

I don't know when I learned that Kimi had married a tall and handsome young man named Terry. Kimi and her husband were living in San Bernardino when Cyndy, who also was living there, came back into Kimi's life. When she learned that Kimi was pregnant with her daughter, Megan, Cyndy often picked her up to take her grocery shopping.

Cyndy was working at San Bernardino County Medical Center as a respiratory therapist when one day she got paged to come to the labor and delivery room. Kimi was in labor and had told the staff to page Cyndy. Cyndy filled in as her birth coach. I knew nothing of any of this until many years later. I must have known Kimi was pregnant. Why wasn't I in the loop? Had I chosen not to be?

I was thirty-six and married again when I reconnected with Kimi. She and her husband had two children. She called me one day and shouted into the phone, "Send diapers now!" and hung up. I didn't call back. I didn't send diapers. I knew

Kimi and her husband were into drugs. Not long after the call, I decided to visit her because I wanted to meet my niece and nephew. Because I felt too nervous and uncomfortable about seeing Kimi again after so many years had passed, I asked a friend from college to accompany me.

Their apartment was on the second floor in a run-down neighborhood, in a shabby apartment building with dried yellow grass, a dark stairwell leading to their apartment. I knocked, and when Kimi opened the door, her face was gaunt; she looked anorexic. I could see behind her the room was dark, the curtain pulled. She was so skinny, so pale, her eyes dull. I knew Kimi and her husband were meth addicts, which explained the turn their lives had taken. Megan was just five years old, a pretty little girl with big brown eyes. Dragging himself across the floor was her son, Austen. I believe he had spina bifida, as his feet were turned upside down. I was horrified and heartsick. His condition could have been corrected, but instead, he ended up in a wheelchair for the rest of his life because both of his parents were so high on meth all of the time that they couldn't get it together enough to take care of his needs. The ramifications of what we had done to Kimi were not lost on me. The trauma transcended the next generation, and we were at fault just as much as anybody else was.

I didn't see Kimi again until I learned she was dying from a rare form of lung cancer. She didn't smoke cigarettes, but maybe it was due to the meth. By this time, Kimi, her husband, and their two children were living with his family: his mother, his stepfather, two or three disabled brothers of his mom, several Chihuahuas, in another dark house, the television droning on, almost everyone on disability.

Kimi had been ill for some time. Her husband and his family considered her a malingerer. Finally, someone in that house decided Kimi needed a doctor. When we learned she was dying, I rushed with my brothers to try to save the day, to save Kimi's children. This didn't go well. Nobody wanted to be saved. Who the hell did we think we were claiming Kimi and her children now?

The day Kimi died, Cyndy brought a beautiful scarf to the hospital and tied it around Kimi's bald head and then put makeup on her. I arrived sometime in the afternoon. Kimi looked pale but beautiful, her eyes determined and brave. She smiled at herself in the mirror. I have pictures, lots of them, with her brothers and sister leaning in beside her, her husband in another. We stayed with her all afternoon and into the evening. At some point, Sandy arrived. We knew Kimi was going to die that night. We were curled around her hospital bed. Suddenly the room grew quiet and still. Kimi's eyes were closed. She was ready to leave us. She whispered, "The time is now," and then she was gone.

Her husband said, "I commend her soul to Heaven."

After Kimi died, my brothers and I tried being part of Austen and Megan's lives. Ron and Cyndy had them over to their house often. They wanted to adopt them. My husband and I picked up Megan for weekend visits. We believed we could prove their father and his entire family were unfit to raise them. The problem was that Megan and Austen didn't want to live with us. They didn't like rules. They didn't like schedules. They didn't like homework. Megan and Austen had no use for the way we lived our lives. Eventually, they all moved to Sacramento, which ended our contact with them.

One day several years ago, I received a letter from Megan in which she told me I was always her favorite and how she regretted she hadn't come to live with Ron and Cyndy. I never wrote back. Cyndy has always kept in touch with Megan, who has had a hard life, had babies too young, worked in a nursing home, and tried to go to school. She is married again and just had another baby. She is happy.

Recently, Cyndy sent me a picture of Megan and Austen from Megan's Facebook page. Austen, sitting in his wheelchair, and Megan, standing behind him leaning into the chair, are beautiful. I am their aunt. Yet through fear and selfishness, I have no relationship with them.

Afterword

One day in the early 1990s, I heard a colleague of mine in the English department at Marymount musing about Joan Didion's "Some Dreamers," weighing the merits of teaching it to his seniors in conjunction with *The Great Gatsby*, both stories about strivers run amok.

I was horrified. I had never talked about that essay—not in high school, not in college—with one exception: my best friend Jill Bickett, chair of our English department, to whom I immediately ran with this information. I feared some student might ask if the "Debbie" in the essay was me, as far-fetched as that would be given the time and distance I'd created from that fourteen-year-old girl. Still, what if an excited student passed on the news to her parents, who would then call the school demanding to know if one of their teachers had been hired without revealing her sullied and infamous past? I would be called in, excuses would be made; the school couldn't be embarrassed this way, and I would lose everything.

I had always known that essay would one day ruin my life, and now it was happening. The situation worked itself out because the teacher ended up not teaching the essay, and I was off the hook, for the time being.

Then, in October 1991, I sat on my pink couch at home in Venice looking through my books on writing for a good descriptive essay describing a place that reflected the author's feelings. I found myself once more reading Didion's essay, and then I read it again. It had, for so many years, caused me to keep silent about my past. I read Didion's descriptions of us, of my mother, and of where we lived through my adult eyes. I saw that what Didion saw and wrote were in fact spot-on.

I was an adult. My mother was dead. Didion was a genius. I was free to have my own opinions. I saw that my mother hadn't fooled Didion. We were a modern-day Joad family. My burdens were lifted.

I decided to write to Didion. I wanted her to know what had become of us. Guy was a dentist. Ron was a high school English teacher. Kimi was dead.

My letter began:

Dear Joan Didion,

I am anxious, angry, and jealous as my fragile self-esteem evaporates. I just can't seem to avoid "Some Dreamers of the Golden Dream." It helped to make you famous, but it's my life.

I anxiously awaited her reply, which arrived six month later. In it, she wrote:

Dear Debra Miller, I've begun this letter so many times, because there's no real way to tell you how moved I was (am) by your letter.

Then, the letter moved away from me and talked about the weird relationship between an author and her subject. She continued:

As a writer I tend to compartmentalize the people and events I've written about—the writer goes in, tries to understand the story, as if the act of writing it down completed the situation, became the truth. I guess I think writers need to do this, have to do this to maintain the nerve to write anything at all. But of course it's an illusion.

I'm glad you wrote to me. Thank you.

Six years later, I had the occasion to meet Didion and her husband, John Gregory Dunne, at the Writers Guild Theater in Beverly Hills. My husband's daughter, Robin, was a *Times* columnist and would be interviewing Didion on stage about her latest novel, *The Last Thing He Wanted.*

Robin let me know that Didion could be aloof and not to expect anything from her. I thought she wouldn't want to have anything to do with me. But that's not what happened. When Robin introduced us backstage, Didion threw her arms around me, called her husband over to meet me, then tucked her arm in mine and escorted me into the auditorium and sat me down beside her. We sat in the audience together while C. Shelby Coffey III read an excerpt from "Some Dreamers," focusing on the moment my father burned to death, and she grabbed my arm and gave it a hug. Years of mortification melted away.

Sometime after that, I told my colleagues at school the long held secret that Ms. Miller was "Debbie," the fourteen-year-old who cried out for her mother when the judge read the guilty verdict. I told my story to each junior English class thereafter, inviting them to ask me anything they wanted. It was a giant relief to have this secret set free.

Today, I'm proud to be the subject of a Joan Didion essay. When I talk about "Some Dreamers," people are usually fascinated. It's part of the reason I wrote this book.

When I heard that Didion died, the loss felt personal. I called my brother Ron to talk about what she had meant in our lives.

If not for her essay, I would not be the woman I am today, a woman inspired to write her own story, a woman who survived and flourished rather than succumb to the darkness that once beckoned me and that consumed my mother.

Acknowledgments

It takes a village to write a memoir.

My Village:

In my early forties, my cousin Suzanne and I were strolling on the beach when she asked me if I had ever thought of writing a memoir. A year later, I was taking a run with my stepdaughter Robin Abcarian, a columnist for the *Los Angeles Times*, and she suggested I write a piece for the *Los Angeles Times Magazine*. "A Mother's Crime" was published April 2, 2006. Robin introduced me to Ardith Hilliard, a retired editor for the *Times*, without whom this memoir would never have been written. I owe everything to Ardith, her belief in my story, her guidance, patience, and compassion as I wept my way through several drafts.

Thank you to my granddaughter Krissa Lagos, who edited the early versions of the manuscript and taught me about the process of publishing. It was Krissa who introduced me to Brooke Warner, publisher of She Writes Press. Thank you to Brooke and my editor Shannon Green for helping me turn my life story into a memoir.

Thank you to Guy, Ron, and Cyndy for your invaluable help with outlining timelines and for sharing your memories that sharpened scenes and ensured accuracies. Guy and I sat and cried as we reconstructed Kimi's story, Cyndy filled in stories of my mom's battle with cancer, and Ron checked on me so many Sundays to make sure I wasn't falling apart. Even as I kept forgetting our discussions or losing my notes, he patiently helped me. I also thank my cousin Tommy, who sent me maps of Wallowa County, photos of our family, and his memories of our grandparents' cabin at Wallowa Lake.

Thanks to my psychiatrist, Dr. Jenny Muller, who sent me on the path to stability so I was able to write my story. And thank you to my dear friends Jill Bickett, Meredith Louria, and Cynthia Colon for their friendship and encouragement through the difficult—and at times, painful—process of writing my memoir.

About the Author

Debra Miller grew up in San Bernardino County, where her mother was convicted of murdering her father when Debra was fourteen years old—the story she chronicles in this memoir, which is her debut work. She taught high school English for thirty-three years at an all-girls school in Los Angeles, California. She is now retired and living in Playa del Rey, California, with her precious cat, Kiki.

Author photo © Cyndy Miller